"Every time I am with a group of Christian laymen, I see not only faithful witnesses but suffering martyrs. They hurt and they endure fiery trials. They listen to me and other sinners preach."

With tongue in cheek, Bishop Gerald Kennedy opens a unique book for and about laymen and the church of which they form so vital a part. In page after page of witty insight culled from years of experience, he distributes warm praise as well as practical advice and warning to lay people concerning the many aspects of their church, its mission, its ministers, and their own participation in its life. These are only some of the topics he covers:

- **Future**
- **Councils**
- **Membership**
- **Youth**
- **Standards**
- **Salaries**
- **Timing**
- **Communication**
- **Denomination**
- **Bulletins**

"You want to see a miracle?" asks Bishop Kennedy. "Look at a church where some are bright and some aren't, some are men and some are women, some are old and some are young, some are rich and some are poor, and they stay together and have amazingly few fights. I can only come to the conclusion that here is a martyr-band both in the active and the quiet sense. They witness and they suffer for their Lord, and I think it is the greatest thing in the world. This is a saving fellowship."

For Laymen
and Other
Martyrs

GERALD KENNEDY

For Laymen and Other Martyrs

1817

HARPER & ROW, PUBLISHERS

NEW YORK, EVANSTON, AND LONDON

FIRST EDITION

LIBRARY OF CONGRESS CATALOG CARD NUMBER: 69-17007

1478894

This is for J. Wesley Hole

Contents

Preface   9

Martyrs

It may sound somewhat farfetched to include laymen in the general category of "martyrs." Even under the worst of conditions, whoever heard of a layman having his eyes gouged out or his limbs broken or his body made into a torch? This must be sheer hyperbole, which is a genteel way of saying that the writer is probably a liar and we had better regard everything he writes like a prosecuting attorney examining a hostile witness. Spurgeon said that "some ministers would make good martyrs: they are so dry they would burn well." Maybe, I hear you say, you have the wrong fellow. How about putting the minister into the martyr's role and leave us alone?

But give me a minute more of your attention. The word "martyr" in Greek shares the same etymological root as the word "witness." How about that? What shall we say about thinking of the layman as a witness? What shall we say about a layman standing for an idea, or following a Man even when it costs him something? And then we ought to consider a man being faithful to a vision when the going is hard and he gets discouraged. Every time a fellow speaks or acts he is bearing witness to some purpose—some value—some cause—and hence, he is a martyr.

Every time I am with a group of Christian laymen, I see not only faithful witnesses but suffering martyrs. They hurt and they endure fiery trials. They listen to me and other sinners preach. They put up with fumbling church bureaucrats who plague us. They listen to pronouncements with which they do not agree. And through all of this and other sufferings, they pay their pledges, eat TV dinners when their wives are late getting home from the Women's Society. They send their children to Sunday School even when the little monsters scream and kick. I tell you, a man does not get his name inscribed in the Lamb's Book of Life easily.

Frankly, I am not surprised that some laymen do not like me. I am astonished that after being their pastor for a few years, any of them will even speak to me. You want to see a miracle? Look at a church where some are bright and some aren't, some are smart and some are stupid, some are men and some are women, some are old and some are young, some are rich and some are poor, and they stay together and have amazingly few fights. I can only come to the conclusion that here is a martyr-band both in the active and the quiet sense. They witness and they suffer for their Lord, and while others may complain about the ineffectiveness, the lack of vital life in the church, I think it is the greatest thing in the world. This is a saving fellowship. Critics, try that on for size. George Bernard Shaw said that "martyrdom is the only way in which a man can become famous without ability." Well, maybe so. The church endures and advances by the faithfulness of ordinary martyrs who are found by Christ and made heroic by his presence.

Our closing hymn is 285 in the old book:

> A glorious band, the chosen few
> On whom the Spirit came,
> Twelve valiant saints, their hopes they knew,
> And mocked the cross and flame;

They climbed the steep ascent of heaven
Through peril, toil, and pain:
O God, to us may grace be given
To follow in their train!

Arise, martyrs, and let us be going.

Hollywood, California GERALD KENNEDY

For Laymen
and Other
Martyrs

I. CHURCH

1. Attraction

Clarence Darrow was a brilliant man and sometimes merely a smart aleck. He said one time: "Depression may bring people closer to the church, but so do funerals." He was voicing the widespread point of view that churches would soon go out of business if it were not for trouble. Lots of people believe this, and there is some evidence to substantiate it. Certain psychologists who know at least as much about the church as a rabbit, say it peddles comfort and that is all.

In times of war we are told that there are no atheists in foxholes. It cannot be denied that the days of depression are better days for the church than the days of prosperity. When a fellow is hard up, he tends to think more about his soul. Many a man who went his way without a thought about God in the sunshine, found himself with a second thought when the storm struck.

Now this is not too bad even if we drop it right there. A good deal of life is in the foxhole, enduring depressions, and getting slapped down by failure. If all we could say about religion was that it is the place we turn to when everything goes wrong, it would certainly demand no apology.

But there is another side to this which Brother Darrow did not see. Men turn to the church not only for funerals but for weddings. Even the boy and the girl who have not been overpious come into the sanctuary when they take this frightening step of promising something to another person for life.

People turn to the church when babies are born. I have been in this business long enough to know how often young couples who have drifted far from their religion come back with their children. Something deep in their lives reminds them of something they had one time which they want their youngster to have. So, back they come and "a little child shall lead them."

Men sometimes turn back to the church when they have to thank something or someone for joy. They haven't thought it through theologically, but suddenly they are aware that they cannot accept gifts they do not deserve without thanking someone. When they begin to think of who they ought to thank, God taps them on the shoulder again.

This means, I suppose, that in the deepest and oftentimes most tragic experiences of our life, the church seems the logical and, indeed, the only place for us to go. And the other side of the picture is that when something happens to us that is so wonderful we cannot find words to express our happiness, nothing will do in that situation but to come back to the altar where we were confirmed in our youth. The church is eternal because in the crucial moments it is the only place where it seems proper for us to speak things too deep and too personal to be said out in the world.

2. Excitement

It is usually a disillusioning experience to see a man twenty to thirty years after he has graduated from college. It is usually disillusioning to see what has happened. His so-called intellectual life which once grappled with new ideas and tough propositions, now is being nourished with daily newspapers and magazines. What happened to the young man who thought that thinking was an important part of life and that being disturbed in mind was as normal as getting up in the morning?

It is a sad thing to see what has happened physically. The college athlete who made it to the Olympics, kept his girth in bounds, and could climb three flights without a collapse. Now he has two layers of flab hanging over his belt, is short of breath, and takes the elevator when he is going up one floor. And then, after you thank God that you are not as other men, you take a look at the mirror and something whispers to you that while he looks like a slob, you do not look so good yourself.

Now this happens to institutions and it happens to the church. Pity! The lean and brave courage of the early church is hard to find except in some rare places. We are fat cats settled down and content if we take the sharp edge off our paganism and give a little sentimental camouflage to our pagan practices. The church has become what we have become and together we have lost our youth, our vigor, our courage, our hope, and now aim merely to protect our investments and die in luxury.

It does not have to happen either to men or to churches. I know one church that makes such demands upon people that it won't let anybody join it unless he knows what he is facing. But there is a vigor in that congregation that is refreshing. The laymen are so committed to the purposes of Christ that they spend time studying about it. They get involved in the events of their town and spend time learning what the ghetto is thinking about and why the ghetto exists. They get criticism from all kinds of people in other churches, and they are regarded by city hall as a dangerous and subversive influence. Subversive to politicians up for reelection, that is.

But a strange thing happens. People are joining all the time, and for every one they lose, they gain five. The services of worship are exciting. They seem to think that Christianity is not an old thing but a contemporary discovery. It is new life, new hope, and new happiness it is offering.

One of the paradoxes of life is that being comfortable gets to be a very boring experience. Pity the congregation that has put this aim first and pity those who make the church only social and respectable. The great thing to note is that not all our best is behind us. When a church takes hold of the problems of its community, what happened in the first century happens again. The gospel has not run out but we have run down. When a high school student said to a preacher, "It is exciting to hear you preach," she was saying something that not many people say to many preachers. When a church becomes an exciting organization, it may not fit the general picture, but that it exists at all means that if you do not have it in your place, you are being shortchanged.

3. Pride

I was walking one Saturday and three children playing in a front yard looked up and smiled. As I went on past, the smallest one, a little boy about five or six years old, said, "We know you." I turned around and went back and asked them how they knew me. The little girl, who was about eleven, said, "We are Methodist children." That warmed my heart as they seemed to be so proud of their church.

There is a curious lack of pride on the part of laymen and ministers about their church. A preacher apologizes for his failure and calls it preaching. There comes from our pulpits too often either bitter denunciation of the institution or a whining self-pity. No one expects the minister to preach a sentimental gospel of sweetness and no one wants a continual pep talk about mother, home, and heaven. But the layman being drenched continually in pessimism tends to look down his nose at an institution which even its employees run down. I tell you it is not very often one hears a glad, confident voice say, "I am a Christian, I belong to this church, and I'm proud of it."

Should we be proud of the church? Well, I don't know anything else that made such contributions to our civilization. Name me if you can any other organization that has lasted, let alone prospered, through the rise and fall of nations and been subjected to the blood and terror of nineteen hundred years. Brother, what else has such a history!

But I feel an even greater pride when I consider its aims. As Chesterton said, "Even a bad shot is dignified when he accepts a duel," and the church has taken on all comers. The church believes in men, in their freedom and in their individual dignity. It judges all systems which try to make life so safe and monotonous that men will not have to be good. Incidentally, hearing such utopias described is about as exciting as watching paint dry.

I stop now and then to think of what the church has meant to me personally, and I am astounded. My life leaves much to be desired. But I will confess that it would have been a hundred times worse had it not been for the church. We have been through some discouraging times in America during these past years. Who has dared to warn and protest and clobber the two-bit demagogues who have made fortunes trying to destroy our freedom and deny our heritage? The church, that's who. After I listen to the Birchers trying to save me, it is the word of the church I turn to with trust.

Blessings on that little girl who is proud of her church. I love her. And blessings on every layman who sees through the defects to the greatness. I love them, too.

4. Sanctuary

There was a Methodist congregation in the north of England a long time ago which got into a row, a most unusual thing to happen in a church. Somebody had the idea they should bring a melodeon into the chapel to help the singing of the hymns. Hymn singing is, or used to be, very important to Methodism. The debate got bitter and finally when the vote was taken, a small majority decided they would try the melodeon. Whereupon one of the stalwart old members left the church in disgust. It was later discovered he was attending the Church of England for worship on Sunday, and one of his former Methodist colleagues asked how he could justify such an action. After all, they had brought only a melodeon into the chapel, while the Church of England had an organ. "Oh," said the old man, "an organ in the Church of England is one thing, but a melodeon in the house of God is another."

Do we still call the church the house of God? Maybe only the old-fashioned people. But there is something significant about this name for the sanctuary. Not that anybody believes that here is the only place God is to be found. We do not think that because certain words have been spoken and a certain dedication made, that this is the place where He will meet us and not somewhere else. But the church is in a special sense truly "a house of God."

For one thing, this is what it was built for. We have used our resources, our imagination, employed men with taste and skill to give us something with an atmosphere of the sacred. When you see a church that looks like a fancy hot dog stand or a new restaurant, you wonder what happened to this impulse. Still, there it is, and the attempt has been made to give us a place that will speak to us of the Almighty.

It is the house of God because significant events transpire in it. Not so much now, but in other times, the church has been the place where we speak our last farewell to the dead. It is the place where our young people stand together and repeat their marriage vows. It is where children and older people are baptized as a sign of their entrance into the Kingdom. It is the place where we listen to a man commissioned and trained to speak to us about eternal issues. This is where the best music we can provide is offered with its universal language of something far beyond our ability to analyze. This is a place of mystery. The Jew in his Holy of Holies did not try to symbolize it but left it empty and dark. And the men who have lost this mystery out of their lives find that their activities are but sounding brass and their lives at the dead end.

Every man needs help in reminding him of who he is and of the awful mystery of God. So whether it is the cathedral, a tent, the plain meetinghouse, or the modern facility sometimes called the "plant," let us remember it is the house of God. That is, if we go there with expectation and humility. And when the French call a hospital *l'hôtel de Dieu*, they have something, too.

5. Future

In 1967 the eminent French sociologist, Raymond Aron, said: "Modern societies are the first ever to justify themselves by their future, the first in which the motto 'Man is the future of man' appears not so blasphemous as banal." With all apologies to this brilliant scholar I must say that the church has from the beginning justified itself by its faith in the future. It says: "Christ is the future of Man." We moderns think of it as an old institution with a long history and a holy heritage. But the church from the beginning put its faith in tomorrow. God, it proclaimed, is not an old idea but a new experience.

Men on the outside are likely to criticize the Christian church because it fails to keep up to date. The critics, however, are inside as well as outside, and they are laymen and ministers alike. Their common complaint is that the church is not listening to the present age and not adjusting itself to the contemporary demands. It is old-fashioned in its methods and out of date in its point of view.

The thing that impresses me most of all as I look at the church from within is its commitment to man and his potential. It sees the new heaven and the new earth, and it talks about the new birth and the new creature. Christianity has been called by somebody "the gospel of another chance." No matter what has happened, there is hope. Back of the clouds in the east there is the promise of a rising sun.

Our world is full of nightmares of what man may become if certain forces have their way. We see man without freedom and man without choice. We see man reduced to automatic responses and forced into the mold of conformity. The future of society under the all-seeing eye of big brother or living in the nightmare of Huxley's "Brave New World" frightens us. I shall be glad to be long gone when and if this nightmare ever becomes real.

But the vision of the future as the Kingdom of God has no such terrifying implications. It is the vision of man becoming truly man and learning more and more love for one another. It is St. Paul's hope for our becoming mature men in Christ. Believe me, it means something to escape from the nightmare visions of the future springing out of science and psychology and sit in a church where the future is envisioned as men becoming brothers and sons of God. Men are homesick for a future, and they find the healing of the homesickness in the vision of the prophets and the saints.

Did you ever hear Methodists sing "The Sweet By-and-By"? They are justifying themselves by their future too much. Better consider that radical book, the Bible. Isaiah quotes God as saying, "I am doing a new thing." Jeremiah joins in with God, talking about "a new law in their hearts." The Fourth Gospel goes the furthest and describes an experience that is like being "born again." St. Paul tells us that in Christ, we are "new creatures." The last book in the Bible describes "a new heaven and a new earth."*

You won't find any society, old or modern, that is anywhere near the church when it comes to justifying itself by the future.

* Scripture quotations, unless otherwise indicated, are from *The Holy Bible*, Revised Standard Version.

6. Councils

Councils of churches in most places do not amount to much. The idea is fine and nobody is going to fault it. But usually when you really get down to cases, if anything is being done in a community it is being done through local churches and local congregations. There is nothing like the conciliar movement to inspire oratory and no action.

This is partly due to the councils' lack of leadership and lack of adequate funds. Still, this is really no answer because what people believe in they work at and what they feel essential they support. I think a more realistic reason is that Christians are usually involved in their own churches, and they do not have enough time or concern to give to another organization when too often it seems like an extra.

This is no attack on councils of churches. I believe in them and I love them. I only confess that I do not believe in them or love them enough to do much about it.

I was thinking the other day that part of the answer to this difficulty is that a church is an association of people who worship together and a council is not. Maybe the worship is the main thing after all. Why can't reasonable Christians of various denominations meet together and plan a united effort for certain projects? Do you suppose the fact that they have not met together regularly in one place for the worship of God is why they do not have the cohesiveness and dedication necessary?

Church life should manifest itself in the activity of Christians in the community. I do not intend to dispute this, but I do raise the question as to whether or not action without worship is enough to live by and enough to save us.

The annual meeting of the Council of Churches is oftentimes a very splendid affair. They have a good speaker and a long program and some pretty good music. But somehow, nobody is personally and directly responsible for the program. Apparently, it is not enough to have people of Christian commitment and goodwill just come together even in the name of the Lord. They have to pray together and listen to the preached word together and experience that strange and wonderful thing which the New Testament describes as happening where two or three are gathered together in His name. I guess this means that when people covenant together to worship regularly, something happens there that can happen nowhere else. Maybe it means that when people grow careless about this part of their religious life, everything goes wrong.

The hymn says:

> We share each other's woes,
> Our mutual burdens bear,
> And often for each other flows
> The sympathizing tear.

This does not happen when we get together casually, say once a year.

7. Arrogance

Fred Allen, one of the great comedians of all time, said: "Some movie stars wear their sunglasses even in church: they are afraid God might recognize them and ask for an autograph." Having lived and done my work in Hollywood for nearly twenty years, Allen's suggestion was not as exaggerated as it may seem to some Americans. The make-believe world of the cinema has produced all kinds of strange and wonderful phenomena. Among them is an inordinate desire to be seen in the right places, speaking to the right people. But above all, it is important to be recognized.

Do not think, however, that this characteristic is unique to Southern California. The Bible calls this common human sin idolatry, which means essentially to put some value or some person in the place of God. It is an occupational hazard of the ministry, and many a preacher falls into the trap of thinking of himself more highly than he ought to think. If he is successful and popular, he had better have a tactful and realistic wife to keep him sane or a good friend in the ministry to speak the truth to him. Best of all is a layman who can appreciate him and at the same time encourage humility.

For the layman the danger is also a real one. It is particularly virulent if the layman is well-to-do and has made some key contributions to the church. I know a man who gave his church a pipe organ and forevermore thought he should call the tunes. It was not said so at the time of the gift, but obviously he considered real strings attached to his generosity which would guarantee him honor beyond his deserving and authority beyond his ability.

On the other hand, I know a layman who is immensely wealthy, and I have yet to see him throw his weight around in any way or indicate that he should have special attention or special consideration. When you see a man like that, you know you are in the presence of somebody whose heart has truly been touched by Christ. For one of the most pernicious temptations is to take an inordinate pride in one's own status and to make an inordinate demand for special recognition. The unconscious arrogance of conscious power is pretty hard to control.

The church is that wonderful institution claiming equality for every man regardless of social status or financial rating. It is the place where the man with no bank account stands on the same level as the tycoon. We do not very often realize this goal, but it seems to me that there is great glory in aiming for it.

We can hardly escape pride when we see what sorry messes some human beings make of themselves. Only a fool could fail to see the difference in the quality of lives. But when we are in the presence of God, all that the best man in the congregation can do is cry out, "God be merciful to me, a sinner." Strangely enough, when that prayer rises out of his heart, his fellow church members begin to take on a higher value and a greater virtue. Even the movie star who is a church member learns to leave off the dark glasses.

II. CONGREGATION

8. Friendship

A common complaint about churches is that they are unfriendly. I have heard some of the brethren take on a long time about a congregation where, unless you are known, you can go in and come out without a friendly word or a friendly greeting. When I was a minister in New England many years ago, there was a church that in the summertime had a sign on its bulletin board: "It is cool inside." Some wit wrote on it one day: "Brother, you said it."

Churches should be friendly places, and no one must ever leave a service feeling that he has been treated rudely. Certainly the pastor of a church has as one of his chief responsibilities the creation of a warm sense of brotherhood in the congregation. For the stranger among us a brief conversation, a handshake, or a sincere expression of interest and concern oftentimes is the difference between life and death. Lonely men or women, seeking they know not what, are usually looking for somebody who cares whether they live or die.

Some churches try to be friendly by putting official "greeters" in the narthex every Sunday morning. They overdo it. You try to get into the service and this fellow and that lady stops you, shakes hands with you, and then passes you on to somebody else. By the time you get past it, you think you have been through a receiving line. You hope you can find a quiet corner in the sanctuary where everybody will let you alone. You did not come here to shake a lot of hands. You came to find something you have lost, and this organized hospitality strikes a phony note.

I remember a man who was a regular attendant at one of my churches. He arrived only a little before the sermon began because, as he put it, that was all he came for. He told me one time he did not like to sing hymns, and he could not stand a lot of Christians practicing their warm welcomes on him. He said he preferred to come late and leave just as soon as the sermon was over to escape all of the social annoyances.

He no doubt was an exception and does not represent the feelings and needs of most people. But I am sure that a friendly congregation never reveals itself through organized hospitality. It does not happen with a "happy time" where everybody stands up if they are from Texas or California. It does not thaw out the meeting by asking everybody to speak first to the one on the right and then to the one on the left. Service-club stuff has its place, but Sunday morning in the sanctuary is a little more than such meetings.

Friendliness springs out of a conviction that all men are brothers in Christ. It dawns on you when suddenly you recognize that God is the Father of all men. Its best manifestation is an atmosphere where the hymns are sung with enthusiasm and the prayers are heard gladly. In a word, it is like a home where people love one another and where every guest feels the healing spirit in his own soul. A greeter never takes the place of the Holy Spirit.

9. Goodness

I wish I were an artist of some kind so that I could create something that would be a worthy symbol of my high respect for the laymen of my church. I do not desire to confine it to one denomination, but I am more familiar with the Methodist than I am with other communions, although I have no doubt that ministers of every church feel the same way. If I were a painter, I could paint a picture symbolizing their greatness, or if I were a sculptor, I could carve something out of marble or wood that would be a lasting memorial to the great laymen I have known. If I were a poet, I could write lines that would immortalize this feeling of affection I have for them. But I must be content with trying to find a few fumbling words to describe my sense of obligation to the laity.

I was thinking that in all the years I have been in the ministry, I have not known more than a half-dozen mean laymen. You find them once in awhile, and because they are such a terrible pain in the soul, they stand out in a man's memory more than they should. Thank God there are so few. There is the fellow who has to be the boss and he tries to dictate what the preacher says. There is the carping critic who goes to every meeting to prevent any action by raising objections to every forward-looking proposal. Why doesn't this fellow ever get sick? He is always present. There is the fellow who is not very important in the business world, but he has found the church a place to exercise some authority and harass his betters. Yet of all the hundreds of men I have known and worked with, it is something to say that not more than about six of them have fallen into these categories to the extent that to remember them is woe.

On the other hand, I think of all the patient, sincere, hardworking, self-sacrificing saints in our churches. I have never had any doubt that in any church where I served there were better saints in the pews than there was in the pulpit.

The preacher learns about the people who are carrying heavy burdens and making no complaint. They put up with all kinds of annoyances every day because they think it is their duty. I never came home from an afternoon of calling on my people that I did not have a new appreciation of the greatness of the folks who make up the Christian church.

For this reason, the ministerial cynics are few and far between. We see the worst of human life, it is true, and anyone who thinks a minister leads a sheltered life ought to follow him around for a week. But if we see the worst, we also see the best. The quiet heroism which goes on continually within the church is its true glory and the foundation of its real greatness.

When I listen to a long tirade about the ineffectiveness of the church and the uselessness of its program, I listen as long as I can find patience. That is not very long. Soon I have to tell the loud-mouthed brother that if he knew as much about the quiet greatness in an average church as I do, he would keep quiet. I have had a few honors given me in my life, but I place none as high as the privilege of being a pastor to the Christian laymen I have known. Hooray for laymen and other martyrs!

10. Straddler

I was talking to a friend one day when a mutual acquaintance came by. We talked with him for a little while, and when he went on his way, my friend said, "There is a fellow who is so anxious not to offend that nothing he says is ever more than an echo of what the majority is saying at that particular time. His first question when he comes into a room is, 'Where is the fence?'" Well, you know what he meant, and he was describing the straddler who would much rather deny he is alive than take a chance on being in the minority.

There are people who make a career of this kind of behavior and who are going to be well-liked by the majority at any cost. Some think this is the essence of Christianity. Not so. In the church especially there is a place for difference of opinion, and in the long run a man with convictions, if he does not get too obnoxious about it, will not only be respected but better liked than the fellow who is a straddler.

There is nothing wrong in having a point of view and giving the impression at the same time that there is room for differing ideas. If personalities are not too abrasive, they help us to sharpen our own beliefs as well as spot the weakness in our assumptions. Convictions only become a pain to a group when the man who has them is too cocksure and too intolerant of men who differ.

One of my laymen who shall always be remembered with affection was a man who oftentimes differed with me. But after I talked with him for awhile, I was certain that I had been in the presence of an honest man who believed what he said. He never spoke behind my back. I have thought sometimes that if I were ever in a fight, I would rather have him on my side than anybody else I knew. For once he had examined an idea carefully and accepted it, you could be sure he would stand by it whether he won or lost.

The church, like the nation, depends on honest critics who must speak their word because of their deep love for the institution. Only the weak and vacillating will resent this and demand that people must agree and flatter. Thomas, the doubter, was also a valuable member of the disciples' fellowship.

The church is not hurt by critics but by men who demand allegiance at any cost. One of the best friends I ever had always made a strong argument against the motion any time the board wanted to raise my salary. Of course, I am glad that usually the majority did not go with him. But somehow I never could get very mad at him. He knew more about me than some of the other brethren and in all probability knew how little I was really worth. And, after they gave me a raise, he never said another word about it. It just goes to show that even when a fellow says no, you can still love him.

11. Youth

Here are lines from Alfred Tennyson, of all people:

> Ah, what shall I be at fifty
> Should nature keep me alive,
> If I find the world so bitter
> When I am but twenty-five?

I read these lines and somehow I began thinking about young laymen.

Now and again you see a church made up primarily of young fathers and mothers and their young families. There is a lot to be said for this kind of a congregation, and it is stimulating for the preacher. Such a church gets things done more quickly than older congregations, and it often has more courage in tackling difficult problems. It has not learned that some of these things can't be done.

The other side of the coin is that such congregations sometimes make big mistakes. They sometimes want only their own kind in the church, and if another person has a different idea, he is usually told politely that maybe he ought to go somewhere else. There is probably less patience and less tolerance in the young than there is in the old.

When I was a young preacher I used to think if I could just get rid of my elderly people, my church could really move. More times than I care to remember I had a great idea which the young fellows thought was great also but which some of the old members of the board questioned. Then I had to wait awhile and answer a lot of foolish questions, and it seemed to me that the whole thing was being held up by age.

Well, I have learned some other things since which I share with you for free. Every church needs youth and every church needs people who are ignorant of the traditions and therefore not unduly bound by them. But do not forget that what older people lack in enthusiasm, they more than make up for in experience. Clemenceau said one time that everything he had learned he had learned after thirty, which is quite contrary to the modern doctrine that nobody over thirty can be trusted.

At any rate, the church is the one organization that is universal. This is the place where the old and the young belong as well as the rich and the poor. It is a place for the brilliant and for the stupid. We are not going to have a society made up of only one segment or the other. And to have a crucible within it in which all men have to work together to find solutions to general human problems is a very good thing. The church, brethren, lets everybody in just as long as each one, young and old, will confess he is not worthy to be in.

Let the older folks welcome the young ones and give them a voice. Let them have places of leadership just as soon as possible. Let the young members learn in a hurry that some of the older ones are more liberal than they are and have sacrificed more for principles than they have been willing to do yet. Let this new fellowship bind us together that to the world we may show a communion that knows neither Jew nor Gentile, neither bond nor free. If you think this means an idealistic kind of life, then you have not been in the church very long. It means conflict and debate and sometimes, I fear, bitterness. But if we endure with our eye on Him, we shall learn more here about solving the general problems of society than will ever be learned at a service club or in a lodge or by forming a political party.

12. Quietness

If you take the time you can occasionally find some pretty interesting material in newspapers. There was a little story in the *Los Angeles Times* the other day which was taken from a St. Louis *Post Dispatch* editorial. It seems that a team of brain chemists at the University of Tennessee has made some interesting discoveries about the chemical basis of pugnacity. The whole thing is summed up by the statement that mice allowed to see other mice fighting began to show those same characteristics an hour and a quarter later. While mice who had not seen the fighting remained quiet and peaceful. It seems that there is a chemical called *norepinephrine* which is produced when a mouse is aroused to fighting pitch. It was pointed out that other studies have shown that under certain conditions the viewing of violence does beget violence. It is probably too much to hope for that a shot of a certain chemical into a small boy or gangster or an international statesman would keep us all sane. It does seem to say, however, that what other people do has an influence on people who see them doing it.

This is old stuff, of course, but now it may be taken with more grace by people who prefer a chemical explanation over a moral one. It is an astonishing thing that the teachings of the Bible and the philosophers all seem so much more certain and believable if we can manage to find some scientific explanation.

I was thinking about this in the church. There are those gifted laymen who speak well and carry considerable authority. On Laymen's Day they are the fellows who fill the pulpit. The impression gets abroad that only the man who can follow in their footsteps is a worthy layman.

I want to tell you about some men I have known who were quite different from these stars of the oratorical world. They speak once in awhile but always quietly and without any fanfare. They fill their places faithfully with their families and they take responsibility when asked. Usually they are not sitting on the platform at a church meeting, however, and their quietness may cause their lay brethren to overlook them. But believe me, the preacher knows them. For by their examples, they bring judgment upon the raucous self-seekers and the publicity hounds who try to make their presence known by some cute remark or some radical suggestion with little truth in it. I believe that their influence pervades the whole fellowship in such a way that were they suddenly to disappear, the whole enterprise would drop ten points.

A fighting champion of empty causes and blown-up phrases looks ridiculous in the light of the quiet witness of these brethren. They are the ones who seem to be saying, "You fellows just need a shot of some chemical to cure you of your empty posturing." Let us give thanks for the laymen whose examples proclaim the peaceful achievements of the devoted fellowship and the quiet glory of the gospel. Somehow we have to find a way to tell the noisemakers that they are suffering a chemical deficiency and that the work of the church is always done by men who, having a full sufficiency of the Holy Spirit, are usually quiet.

III. INSTITUTION

13. Standards

It is interesting to note that people expect so many more things from the church than they do from other institutions. In a commercial relationship they take some things for granted, but if the same thing happens in the church, they are very much upset. Nobody gets offended when a store sends you a bill at the end of the month. But I have known Christian church members to get all upset because the church sent them a reminder of their pledge and how much was owing.

I remember a satire I read a long time ago about a man who said he was no longer attending the local movie theater because the manager never called on him. He was through with it because the folks weren't friendly in the theater. At once it became clear to me again of how we expect some things from our brethren in the church that we don't expect from them in any other place.

Now this is both good and bad. It is bad because we make impossible demands and expect people to be different on Sunday from the rest of the week. We think that if a man is in a church, he ought to be a different kind of man and that we ought to receive different treatment there from anywhere else. We raise impossible expectations to what will happen and what ought to happen. But it is good that we recognize the church as a beachhead of the Kingdom of God. We see it as a colony of heaven or a fellowship showing how the world's ills can be healed. Even when the most impossible demands are made upon it, I always say to myself that it certainly indicates the high place the church occupies in the minds of most men.

Let the Christian layman remember this in his behavior and in his thought about the church. It is not enough that he should be just a fairly honest person in his relationships, or at least fairly moral in his standards. Something more is expected and demanded. Not that he should have a double standard, but his membership in the church should remind him constantly of what he ought to be at all times.

This I think is one of the great contributions the church makes to human society. It creates an environment that tempts us to be better than we usually feel like being. We are told of a fellowship dedicated to strengthening the weak and comforting the sorrowful. We are for a time thrown into an atmosphere of kindness and love. Great issues are placed before us for consideration, and eternal matters are on our minds.

A man speaking of a beloved physician said that whenever he entered the room, "I made up my mind to get well." This is the influence of our Lord, and when that influence comes to us through the preacher and through the presence of our brethren who are his servants, some of the sick things in our lives disappear. We make up our minds we are going to be and do well. You see, the truth is that the church exerts so many indefinable and unobservable influences that we are oftentimes being healed by it imperceptibly. Sometimes we never learn about these things until we have lost them.

14. Salaries

It is the layman's task to be aware of the business affairs of his church, and that includes the salaries of the minister or ministers. In the business world this is a fairly simple matter, and it is assumed that every man will get the most he can command. Salaries go with the job, and the more important the job, the more generous the salary. It is not quite like that in the church. Let a minister even hint to his laymen that he ought to have so much and he is branded immediately as a money-mad fiend more interested in dollars than in souls. Believe me, it is a very ticklish situation.

Now, nobody in the church, if he has any sense at all, thinks that the salaries are going to be the same as they are in the corporation. There was a time when it was assumed that schoolteachers were more or less in the same sad predicament as the ministers when it comes to salaries. But even educational institutions now give what seems to the poor preacher an astronomical salary to a fellow whose responsibility is less exacting than his. If a man goes into a church, he goes moved by motives other than getting rich.

But the astounding thing to observe is that when laymen get into the business affairs of the church, they sometimes take on an entirely new point of view. I wish I could believe it was an extra conscientiousness in spending the Lord's money wisely. It usually, however, is a human trait to take advantage of a fellow if you can.

The result is that salaries are kept to a minimum and raises are given very painfully.

Let me give a radical point of view here, although, as I have suggested, it is accepted as commonplace economics in business. The small salary is the most expensive one. In this field, as in practically all fields, you get what you pay for, and the man who works for very little will cost the church so much money that one really cannot afford to have him around. Sometimes the cheapest thing a church board can do is to pay an adequate salary for an adequate minister. Let the layman apply to this part of his responsibility the biblical injunction that it is more blessed to give than to receive.

I know many ministers and I know hardly any in the profession for the money. But I know also that when the church gives a fellow a raise at the end of the year, it says to him in loud and clear tones: "We like what you are doing and you have our enthusiastic support."

You cannot make a poor minister a good one just by raising his salary. But you can make a good one even more effective by showing some financial appreciation regularly. Appreciation gives any man an extra enthusiasm. But who am I to be teaching you fellows economics? Come to think of it, however, it is not so much economics as psychology. I would even go so far as to say that it is practical Christianity.

15. Slowness

A common complaint of laymen is that the church is too slow in doing what ought to be done. Businessmen are in the habit of making decisions and implementing them. In the church you have to deal with committees and boards which are fine if they do not give the impression that their main purpose is delay. The Irishman who said, "I'd rather walk ten miles than stand one," is speaking the mood of many laymen. Give us something to do, they say, and show us some action and then maybe we can get more enthusiastic about the church.

Now let it be said that this is a good mood, often justified, and the church takes an unconscionably long time in doing its work. The layman who lives his life within its walls soon learns that what might take a year at most in his business will probably take five years or more in the church. Patience, brethren, is one of the necessary virtues for churchmen. How often it seems to us that there is nothing in society to compare with Christianity when it comes to slow motion.

But like most things, there is another side to be considered. For one, the church is made up of all kinds of people and hardly ever are they like-minded. You may have a congregation now and then that has deliberately limited itself to one kind of person or one point of view. These are not congregations representing the Christian church. The minister learns that he is a leader of people who come from every strata of society. They are young and old;

they are rich and poor; some are bright and some are not. But then, so is society, and if the church can finally find a basis of action and unity of spirit in Christ, its forward move will carry more influence than when the American Legion or the PTA agrees on a program.

Another thing to be considered is that society certainly needs some conserving institutions to make sure that we do not throw baby out with the bath. Today, in particular, the worship of youth and a preference for enthusiasm as a substitute for age and experience are the order of the day. Do not be too ready to write off something that has been around for over two thousand years and has proved able to put its roots down in nearly every society and nation. This is not the most spectacular part of its work, but this is something men need. When a fellow gets weary of changing styles and fads, it is rather comforting to be in touch with something that won't be out of style next year.

Stalin's reply to the suggestion of the Pope's importance was: "How many battalions does he have?" Not many battalions but a great deal of influence and power. It takes a long time to establish something that can endure on the basis of free-will offerings. So keep the pressure up on the church that it does not go to sleep or lag unnecessarily. But be glad that if the church is difficult to move swiftly and immediately, it is also mighty hard to destroy. You may need this quality in your own life sooner than you think, and you will discover that where you develop fortitude best is by being a member of something dedicated to the worship of one who is "our help in ages past, our hope for years to come."

16. Tents

David in the time of his prosperity and triumph wanted to build a house for God. He felt guilty living in a palace while only a tabernacle was provided for the Lord. But the prophet Nathan came to him and said that God did not want David's plan because "I have not dwelt in a house since the day I brought up the people of Israel from Egypt to this day, but I have been moving about in a tent for my dwelling" (II Sam. 7:6). This does something to our cathedral psychology—our edifice complex. It does something to our static theology. The trouble with the cathedral is that it is so permanent. It is established and you cannot move it. It gives the impression that we have arrived and the journey is ended.

It takes an old, old book to remind us that God moves with the people. He goes ahead and points the way. He was in Israel's battles and disputes. They were a people on their way to claim a promised land, and the God who made that promise was leading them. This is a word for us.

Some of the modern rebels insist that cathedrals are all wrong and that the church ought to spend its money for the poor and the depressed. But we are not going back to the church in the house of the first century because the Christian church is something different today and so is our society. We must have facilities to carry out the Lord's commandments, and we need centers for the life of the congregation. But the static church will not serve this period either.

The task for Christians is to note that God was later willing for Solomon to build the temple, but he expected even Solomon to remember that the tent was and must always be the symbol of His spirit. Out of the temple we go into the ghetto, into the parks and onto the streets as the evangelical preachers did in the eighteenth century. There is nothing wrong with the cathedral until we begin to think of it as a tomb. Let us regard it as a wayside shrine where we pause to be refreshed and receive new marching orders. It is neither the end of the rainbow nor the conclusion of the pilgrimage. Think of it rather as a rest stop and a hostel. Tomorrow we must hit the road again for the One whose sign is the pillar of fire by night and the pillar of cloud by day.

Temples can become dens of thieves. They can be insulated, sound-proof mausoleums. Better think of them as stone tents. You cannot fold them up in the morning, but nowadays, the world camps on our front lawn. Just make sure windows are open so we can hear Him tell us what the next step of the journey must be.

17. Denomination

It is a day of the ecumenical spirit and the ecumenical approach. Changes have taken place in the Catholic Church which I never supposed I would ever see in my lifetime. There is a new spirit of fellowship and understanding between the various communions that is exciting and electrifying. The local church sees itself not in isolation but as a part of the Christian church in all its variety and majesty. The lid has been taken off and now those who have changed their minds cannot put it on again. Remember Humpty Dumpty.

Some of us who have been brought up in a particular communion have learned to love it but now feel hesitant to mention it out loud anymore. Has the time come when we must apologize that we are Catholics or Methodists or Quakers? We want to be Christians, but we do not want to give the impression to anybody that we are narrow or sectarian.

I was reading some letters the late C. S. Lewis had written to a friend in America. Lewis was a Church of England member and an English scholar who had been converted to Christianity when he was twenty-nine years old. He wrote a number of fine books about Christians and their religion. In one of his letters to this friend he says: "I believe that, in the present divided state of Christendom, those who are at the heart of each division are all closer to one another than those who are at the fringes. I would even carry this beyond the borders of Christianity: how much more one has in common with a *real* Jew or Muslim than with a wretched liberalizing, occidentalized specimen of the same categories."

This is an unusual insight and I think a very important one. He is saying that we do not become better Christians by becoming poorer Presbyterians or Episcopalians. We do not serve the Christian cause by speaking well of all churches except our own. The unity we seek comes out of committed lives hard at work in some particular denomination. If we are on the outskirts of our particular church or, as he puts it, "at the fringe," we shall not minister to divided Christendom with anything like the power we will possess if we are at the center of a particular communion. We must not, in other words, become the kind of ecumenical people who seem to love the church in general but no church in particular.

Generalities have no power to inspire or stimulate. The abstraction will leave us dull and untouched and bored nigh unto death. It is the concrete instance of Christ at work in the world and of his followers undertaking some precise project for the Kingdom that makes the world better. Let us not get lost in a philosophical and theological underbrush of ecumenicity. Let us realize that our service and contribution are to be given in some particular place within the framework of some particular fellowship.

Thus endeth the lesson.

18. Reality

When I was a Sunday School boy, I remember it was assumed by my parents that all children ought to go to Sunday School and that older people who had nothing else to do probably ought to go also. In between these extremes were parents who had a hundred and one other interests. They had done their duty if they went to church. I do not know whether or not that has now changed very much. But in those days Sunday School was mainly for the very young and for the very old.

I was recently talking with a fellow who told me that in his church one of the most hopeful developments was a class of young married couples who were studying theology. This was not any emotional, soft approach but an attempt to confront the hard and mysterious questions of living and dying which the church wrestles with and seeks an answer. They met every week for a session that demanded preparation and homework.

Then, not very long after that, I met another fellow who told me about a group of businessmen who were meeting for an early morning breakfast once a week. They were discussing some rather tough theological problems, and after a number of weeks there was no sign of any loss of enthusiasm.

It is a radical idea to some ministers that laymen want the church to treat them like adults. It is also a very strange idea to some of the old-timers that laymen should be interested not only in theology but in the latest word concerning biblical criticism.

When I was a young preacher, it was thought that you had to keep these things hidden from the old-timers lest they get upset and lose their faith. Many a young preacher trying to be honest with his own conviction and at the same time not upset anybody's old-time religion, found it difficult to travel the rough road of truth. As a result, one of my old professors used to say that we have taken such good care of our weak brethren that they are about all we have left.

Laymen who are worth their salt know that if their religion means anything at all it must deal with ultimate values of life. It is therefore not to be watered down for babes but given to men in all its challenge and all its reality. Maybe it is time to go back to Sunday School again and have competent religious leaders teach some classes to men and women who are tired of drinking the milk of the gospel and want some meat.

I have no doubt that this process will offend some of the tender-minded lambs of the congregation. I have a belief that for every one we lose we will gain five. Joseph Wood Krutch said one time that people with the power of decision and yet incapable of any sustained attention put our society into a parlous condition. Allow me to say that a church claiming to have the answer to the world's problems and yet not being able to give its members more than a watered-down cream-puff interpretation of the religion of the Cross, better not claim to have the answer to anything. Rise up, O men of God, on Sunday morning or some other morning, and insist that you be privileged to deal with the really tough ones.

IV. MINISTRY

19. Timing

Someday I may write a book on the most unforgettable laymen I have known. When I do I shall certainly mention the fellow who I always thought had the gift for saying the right thing at the wrong time. He was a good man and he had high standards. He was honorable and dependable. But he did not have very many close friends because I suppose he did to them what he always did to me. He was forever speaking a biting, bitter word at a time when I could hardly stand it.

He put in long hours at the church, and he was there on Sunday morning shortly after I arrived. Those moments just before the service are very precious ones to the preacher. At least, they always are to me. But this fellow usually had to see me about something ten minutes before it was time to go into the pulpit. He would point out something he had discovered that was really wrong in the organization, or he had observed something in the physical plant that had to have immediate attention. He had to tell me about it at that very moment. Sometimes he had on his mind something that I had not done very well or something that I had said that would have been better unsaid.

Now I am out to make it clear that I hardly ever disagreed with him, for usually there was some truth in even his most bitter word. But why did he have to speak it just before the service? How did he ever find that evil ability to approach a man just at the wrong time?

Have you ever thought how important timing is in everything that we do? Jesus came, says St. Paul, in "the fulness of time." Our Lord's ministry is marked by a fine sensitivity to the proper moment. He seemed to know when a man needed comfort and when he was able to stand the hard word. This layman was not one of his company.

Says the preacher in Ecclesiastes 3:1: "For everything there is a season, and a time for every matter under heaven. . . ." Then he goes on to talk about a time for killing and a time for healing, a time for winning and a time for losing, a time for weeping and a time for laughing. The good layman as a part of his ministry learns this in dealing with his preacher. Not at the close of the service, my brother, is the time for criticizing the sermon. Wait a little while and talk it over in a more comfortable place. Preachers need the truth spoken to them in love by members of the common enterprise. No one can deny that. Ah, but the timing is all-important.

I have known ministers who were great and good men but who were always in trouble because they said the right thing at the wrong time. And I have also known laymen who were great and good men but whose approach was about as welcome as the plague simply because you could be sure that if they had something unpleasant to say, they would find the worst possible time to say it. What is the answer? Perhaps only the Lord can guide us here, and we ought to speak to Him in prayer. A general rule would be that if you are in doubt, wait awhile. And above all, make sure it is done in private.

20. Encouragement

I went to a church as a new pastor one time long ago in a different part of the country and in a strange city. I was lonesome and I was homesick as always happens to me in such a circumstance. Like every church, it had some problems I had not been told about and some of them seemed either unsolvable or so tough that they would be with me forever. The days passed, and I cursed myself for ever having left the old place and plunged into this foreign field. My wife gave me what comfort she could, but I tell you it was hard going and very discouraging.

The one thing that saved me was a great layman in that new church who never failed to call me every Monday morning. He always began with about the same words: "Doctor, that was one of the greatest sermons I ever heard that you preached yesterday morning." Well, that was always a good beginning and a word I never get tired of hearing no matter how many times it is repeated. I would ease off from the tension a little bit and settle back in my chair. Then this man would go on: "We are lucky people to have you here and you will have a great ministry. Already things are happening that I did not expect to see for many years." Then after conversation back and forth, he would come to the conclusion of the conversation by saying: "Now is there anything I can do for you? Do you need anything? Have we forgotten anything we ought to be doing? Remember," he would add, "we want you to be happy." Well, I would say to myself, "This isn't so bad after all and it is a wonderful thing to be pastor of a church like this one."

Now I am sure that the man took some liberties with the truth. It may be that he sensed I was discouraged and homesick. I know that not everybody would have agreed with him if he had put it to a vote. But I always think of him as a symbol of a great layman who was a minister to his pastor.

Laymen sometimes do not understand how desperately in need of encouragement the minister is. It would be a good thing to remember that if you have any words of encouragement, speak them to him often. When St. Paul and his companions came to Antioch in Pisidia, he went to the synagogue on the Sabbath. After the scripture readings, the chairman of the congregation said to them, "Brethren, if you have any word of encouragement [the word used by several of the newer translators] for the people, say it" (Acts 13:15). There are enough people who tell us the discouraging things. Just one man who stands by through the difficult and lonely times can keep another sane and hopeful. I know a good many preachers and most of them remember how at a particularly crucial time some man said something to them that made them resolve to go on a little longer. And most successful ministers, if they should be asked what has been most important to them in their careers, would probably reply, "Why, I had a layman in my church who always seemed to know when I was really low and he spoke the encouraging word." And let us hope and pray that the minister will do that for you.

21. Character

Somewhere a good long time ago I saw a cartoon showing a young man and a girl confronting an older man and woman who were apparently the girl's parents. The young man was saying, "I make twenty thousand dollars a year. What difference does it make whether I have character?" Perhaps there is just enough truth in it to make us stop a moment and think and perhaps just enough reflection of our time in it to trouble us.

I have made a discovery, and because I am a little on the stupid side it has taken me longer to find this truth than it should have taken. I pass it along to you, although you probably do not need it. But for the slower brethren like me, it may be of some benefit. I have discovered that it does not matter what else a man may have, if he does not have character, he has nothing.

I have had to deal with people in my job who usually assume they must put their best foot forward. The laymen who talk to me usually do not swear or tell dirty stories. The preachers who come into my office are not at any pains to tell me their weaknesses or their failures. But even in this slightly artificial atmosphere, I have learned that there is no way of covering up for very long what the real man is. If you want a text for this meandering, take this one: "Now if any one builds on the foundation with gold, silver, precious stones, wood, hay, stubble—each man's work will become manifest; for the Day will disclose it, because it will be revealed with fire, and the fire will test what sort of work each one has done" (I Cor. 3:12–13). St. Paul is talking about character as the foundation of achievement.

I have a friend who has grown a little cynical in the episcopacy, and he tells me that whenever a fellow begins to talk too long and too loud about being "spiritual," the bishop usually puts his hand on his wallet. He is simply referring to men who make pious talk a substitute for ethical behavior. We have some of them in the church, no doubt, but not very many.

Take it all and all, you will find more people in the church that are good and dependable than you will find anywhere else. There is something about prayer and worship that makes it difficult for a man to live with his hypocrisy. The hypocritical stubble he tries to use as a foundation begins to appear for what it is. Whenever I hear any man sounding off against the church, I want to remind him that it is a wonderful thing to have a company of men gathered together once a week to let the sharp light of God penetrate the dark places of their hearts. We have "characters" in the church, but our chief product is character. And that, my friends, is something not to forget.

22. Infallibility

I see by the papers that the Pope has come out in favor of no chemical or mechanical birth control devices for Catholics. I hear also that not only many Protestants but some Catholics are objecting to this announcement and that even some Catholic theologians have dared to suggest that in their judgment the Pope's ruling is not the word of God.

Well, I have gotten over feeling any sense of rejoicing when any church gets into some difficulty and falls under criticism. At the end of the day, we all stand or fall together, and nothing benefits my church that hurts yours. But I think that a comment or two about what this means may be in order.

If you regard yourself as infallible about anything, you are certainly going to be in trouble when you change your mind. You do not dare say that you made a mistake and that things are different now. That certainly means the end of the infallibility theory and it knocks every man off his infallible throne. About the best you could do if you are caught in this trap would be to make a long, involved statement. Double talk will ease the former pronouncement without actually denying that it was ever wrong. This is a hard trick, but it can be done if you try it. Politicians have been doing it for years, and so have some preachers.

Your only other alternative, it seems to me, is to stand by your ancient pronouncement let come what may. The world may be destroyed by overpopulation, but you must still insist that everybody ought to have all the babies possible and that to limit families is evil. You have to repudiate science which seems quite united in telling us that the earth's space is limited and even flying to the moon is not going to solve the population pressure. The food experts are united in proclaiming that we cannot increase our numbers indefinitely without more and more people starving. More starvation means more conflict and more war.

Perhaps we had better just come to the conclusion that men are not infallible and that we all see through a glass darkly. Perhaps Protestants are on the right track when they regard their ministers as subject to the same temptations as laymen and liable to mistakes in judgment like every sinner. The voice of the layman is very important in the church and so is the voice of the preacher. Let them trust each other and respect each other. May the good Lord deliver us from an infallibility complex either on the part of the man in the pulpit or of the chairman of the board.

In the meantime, let us all pray for the Pope and for our Catholic brothers and sisters. And let us gladly learn from one another, for we never know when God's voice may be coming to us through the expressed opinion of someone not in our church. But infallibility, I am convinced, is a trap.

23. Messenger

My long-time friend, the late Bishop A. Frank Smith of Houston, used to say that a preacher's wife had a harder job than any other wife. She has to live with a man during the week and regard him as the voice of God on Sunday. While that is particularly true of the preacher's wife, the layman is caught in the same difficulty. How does a man deal with another man in society or in business and still think of him as God's special spokesman? For we have never subscribed to the doctrine that the office automatically gives a preacher either special authority or sanctity. This may be a more difficult dogma, practically speaking, than to subscribe wholeheartedly to the mystery of the Trinity.

For the layman who really likes his minister the problem never confronts him acutely. You like a fellow and you assume that what he says and what he does is pretty nearly all right. Even when he says the wrong thing or does the wrong thing now and then, the friendly layman will say to himself that even Jove nodded or Atlas shrugged and in any case every man has a right to a few mistakes. But if the relationship is not a warm personal one, what shall a man do about the voice from the pulpit which so often contradicts the layman's deep convictions?

I expect the best thing he can do is to remember that God speaks through critics as well as through friends. If we have found grace enough to believe that it is possible that we could be wrong, we may even be willing to assume that when that man in the pulpit irritates us the most, it may be God's way of striking us with a new idea or a new perspective. An enemy may be God's spokesman.

Indeed, if we are listening to a man who never says anything to upset us or make us mad, perhaps we ought to examine our souls and look afresh at our own church. It seems to me to be a proper reason for complaint to the pulpit committee or to the bishop if the preacher speaks only to my point of view or prejudices and never says something to upset my peace of mind. The prophet's lash needs to be felt now and again as well as the gentle touch of the shepherd's crook.

I am too much the victim of my own environment and my own heredity. I choose my friends too much from people who agree with me. Maybe it is the good Lord's will that on Sunday morning the man who knows something about the other side of the track and life in the ghetto should be called by God to stab me awake even though it hurts. Let all the laymen say Amen!

Prophets never win any popularity contests. Critics are seldom the artists' best friend. Shepherds frustrate the sheep. But health depends on the surgeon and woe unto us if we prefer an ignorant comfort to an honest disturbance. And often that poor fellow in the pulpit does not enjoy saying it any more than we enjoy hearing it.

24. Amateur

In the Christian scheme of things the layman is an amateur. I do not mean this as in any way derogatory but as the highest compliment. The professional is the fellow that learns to do something well, and he is paid for it or he makes a living out of it. The minister is the professional. The amateur, on the other hand, does something like paint or play the violin or watch birds or get active in the PTA just because he loves it. He will not make any monetary profit from it, but he has found something that so intrigues him that he gives his life to it with a glad abandon.

It is a pity that in our time the day of the amateur seems to be largely over. There are not many families who gather around in the evening for a concert, with each child playing some instrument and father and mother a part of the show. We have the hi-fi where the turn of a switch can bring some professional in to sing for us or play. There are probably some advantages to this, but there are some great losses also. In a day when there was less sophisticated entertainment available, people had to entertain themselves and they learned to do some things just for fun. That is nearly over with us and it is a pity.

The Christian church at its best is an amateur organization. The early disciples were all laymen and so were the early missionaries. The church did not spread across that ancient world because the Board of Missions sent out ordained men. It spread because a Christian layman who traveled somewhere bore witness to his faith as he followed the trade routes. The Christian travelers in the early centuries were the church's missionaries.

In our time we think we discovered something new in emphasizing a layman's work in the office or the factory or the farm. It is as old as the church and is simply going back to something that we have neglected and need to recapture. You cannot hire enough people to do the necessary work of saving the world. You cannot put enough people on the staff of your church to make it alive and vital. Finally, this all depends upon the "amateurs" or the laymen whose hearts have been touched and filled with the unsearchable riches of Christ and who have to tell about it.

A church is like collegiate sports and may sometimes be tempted to hire professionals to play its games for it. But that is not what intercollegiate athletics is supposed to be. Make it a professional affair and you discover one day that it has taken over the academic life as well and made the whole thing a commercial transaction. It is when students play the games for the joy of it that the college remains a learning institution.

We have to have a few pros around, no doubt, but woe unto the church when it becomes a professional affair. And when a man tells me what the Lord has done for him not because the church pays him to do it but just because of love in his heart, that really gets to me. The church must halt the decline of the amateur and restore him to his proper place. That is called rebirth and a renewal.

V. ORGANIZATION

25. Joining

Simone Weil, French mystic and writer, once made a remark about the church which was probably exaggerated. She said, "I should be more willing to die for the church, if it should ever need one to die for it, than to join it." Not being much of a joiner myself, I feel considerable sympathy for her point of view. Still, I am not sure that it would be better to become a martyr than to suffer as a member.

However, I am thinking of church members and of laymen in general. I suspect there are times when they would seriously consider these alternatives in the light of their church experience. I feel called upon to address myself to their condition. If there is little hope of curing it completely, at least I may bring some alleviation of the pain.

The great disillusionment sets in when a fellow discovers that the church is not greatly different from other organizations. This is a shocking experience because he assumed that becoming a part of a holy fellowship would make every member kind of holy. It seemed that just taking the vows and openly confessing one's faith would work a certain amount of change in life. But it is more like Moses coming down from the mountain where he had talked with God and finding the people worshiping a golden calf. It is the disciples on the Mount of Transfiguration. They are led back to the village where a father with a broken heart sought and did not find healing for his son from the disciples.

I tell you it is mighty hard when one discovers that the committees are just as inefficient and tiresome in the church as they are in the lodge. The machinery creaks the same way and bores talk just as long about nothing. Petty minds are still petty and gossipy people usually try to give their poison a little gospel sweetness, but it is still poison.

Then there is the morning worship service. Most churches give you a choice as far as time is concerned. But if it is unbuttoned and flat at eleven, it will not be much more exciting at nine-thirty. It is too bad, but sopranos who give their hearts to Jesus can still be flat or too loud. The good man in the pulpit was not made into a genius when the Commission on Ministerial Qualifications accepted him as a candidate for the ministry. The ushers strut and bring people in at the wrong time and are about as sensitive as truck drivers. So the layman in weariness and despair says to himself, "Whether I die for it or join it, in either case I am a martyr."

Courage, brother, do not stumble, as the hymn admonishes us. The grace of God comes to us through earthen vessels, in St. Paul's phrase. And the church is an earthen vessel. Our trouble is a sentimental idea that religious things are out of this world. Not so! But you will glimpse a flash of beauty here or an unexpected bit of greatness there that makes your heart sing. Suddenly, you will find a saint in the next pew and the earthly weariness will fade away before a heavenly inspiration. Just get over the idea that churches are supernatural gatherings of sanctified angels. Regard them as schools where sinners learn to recognize the greatness behind the ordinary and the heroes behind the voters. Best of all, you may see that salvation is more a matter of faithfulness than it is of entertainment. Now as we sing the last hymn, come down to the altar where you belong and commit your gifts, your prayers, your presence, for another year of service.

26. Membership

What should a church do about taking in new members? Should it be hard or should it be easy? Or should it be somewhere in between? You can find all kinds of opinions and any variety of points of view.

I know a church, for example, that won't take anybody in unless they enroll in a six-week course. The advantage of this method is that everybody has to give it some thought and everybody has to know what he is doing. There is no place here for a man to get a sudden idea that he wants to become a part of the church and make a new start right now. He just has to wait until he has taken the course and learned the requirements.

On the other hand, there are some churches where they just give an invitation and anybody can get up and come right down and become an instant member. Nobody explains anything and nobody asks any questions.

There are plenty of arguments for both ways. Surely, anything as important as becoming a part of the Christian church ought not to be entered into unadvisedly but discreetly and in the fear of God, as the marriage ceremony has it. It affords a wonderful opportunity to educate people as to what a particular denomination and a particular church of that denomination stands for and expects of its people. It eliminates the idea that it is a haphazard, meaningless kind of decision with no real significance.

But there are times when something happens to a man all of a sudden. He may hear a sermon or a prayer or some music that crystallizes half-thought-through and vague inclinations into a demand for concrete action immediately. There ought to be some way that he can stand up and say, "I am going to do something about this and I am going to do it right now." One of my friends said that the reason the early Christians were so suspicious of St. Paul after his conversion was that he had not been through the membership class.

As I look back on my own church and its attitude during the great days of revival under John Wesley, it seemed willing to take anybody in but it was hard to stay in. Those Methodists assumed that the door was wide open to the fellow who thought he needed something the church could give to him. But he was supposed to grow in faith and grace. He was supposed to be a witness and to work at his religion. If this didn't follow, they put him out.

Is this not the best way for a church to look at membership? Anybody comes in the moment he feels he should, and then it is up to that fellowship and the minister to help this new member become a full-grown and mature Christian. Do not keep him out until he proves worthy, for the church is for sinners. Do not deny the possibility that the Lord can speak to a man right now. But if this new member grows cold and careless, help him go somewhere else lest he infect the others. You won't be doing him any harm and it will do the fellowship much good.

27. Bulletins

If there is one thing this age knows a lot about, it is how to advertise. Advertising has become an art, and some of the products of the advertiser are indeed beautiful to behold. Not only that, but they show a real grasp of the principle of salesmanship. Listen to these words that young Aldous Huxley wrote when he was starting his writing career on the staff of a British magazine called Vogue. He wrote: "I have discovered the most exciting, the most arduous literary form of all, the most difficult to master, the most pregnant with curious possibilities. I mean the advertisement. . . . It is far easier to write ten passably effective sonnets, good enough to take in the not too inquiring critic, than one effective advertisement that will take in a few thousand of the uncritical buying public." That is testimony enough from one of the top minds and one of the ablest literary men of the modern world.

With all this knowledge and all these resources with us, why do churches so often turn out a mimeographed bulletin with all the reader appeal of stock market quotations for the fellow who does not own any stock? Not only is it mimeographed but it is poorly mimeographed. It is the kind of sheet busy men throw into the wastebasket immediately without even looking at the heading. This is done in the name of saving the Lord's money for more important things. It is about as stupid a money-saving device as anybody ever dreamed up.

The first relationship of the stranger with the church is the bulletin. The first impression is received from that sheet. If there is one place where we should not try to save money but to do a good job, it is in the document we give to the members of the congregation to guide them as they worship God and tell them what is going on in the church.

The minister may be out of touch with the times. But why do the laymen allow this to happen? I know a church with a top advertising man on its board and a bulletin that he would be ashamed to see used as an interoffice communication medium. Sometimes a smart layman gets pretty stupid when he is thinking of the church. At the very minimum let us be as wise and imaginative for the Lord as we are for ourselves.

I do not claim that an attractive bulletin will fill the church. That still demands a preacher and a choir. But I do claim that changing that blurred, unreadable mess to a sharp, clear, artistic presentation of the church's worship and activities may be the beginning of a new spirit of life and pride.

A rough exterior may hide a heart of gold, if I may coin a phrase. But the worshiper on Sunday morning has neither the time nor the inclination to investigate. Put the gold on the outside.

28. Ushers

Some time ago I was going to a new post. I was in the city the Sunday before I had to start the new job, and I went to church in another denomination to hear a man preach I had heard about. It was a miserable experience and I will tell you why.

We arrived at the church just a little late, which was the reason for what followed. The usher at the door was a sourpuss and had apparently received his training, if any, as an army sergeant or a prison guard. He put those of us who were waiting to get into the church in our place in a hurry, and he did it with no grace whatsoever. We were told to stand over there and get out of the way, and then we were told where we could sit. There was not the slightest feeling of welcoming a guest to the Father's house, but a regimented procedure to get us in the sanctuary with a general attitude of resentment that we were there at all. By the time we were seated in the pew, I was so inwardly stirred up that I never did get back into a proper atmosphere of worship.

For the first time I realized how tremendously important ushers are in the church. If a man is called upon to be an usher, let him rejoice that he has been called upon to take one of the key positions. It is obvious when you stop to think about it that the first personal relationship a stranger has is with the usher. The first impression that the visitor receives is from the way the usher acts and does his work. Why churches neglect this important thing and treat it without proper concern is a mystery. Probably just ignorance and thoughtlessness.

I do not think it makes very much difference whether the usher is young or old. There is probably a place in every church for young men to be introduced to this service and to have some training. But the waiting worshiper is not overimpressed just because a fellow is under thirty, nor will he give it a second thought if he is over sixty. But one thing is sure in my mind: he will be tremendously impressed by the way the job is done and whether or not he feels any sense of Christian welcome in the usher's behavior.

If I were pastor of a church, I certainly would not take a man for this job just because he had a dark suit and was available. I would give this matter careful thought, and I would certainly recruit the brethren with care and discrimination. This is the house of God, my friends. Think what kind of a man is worthy of being the voice of welcome in such a place.

There is a biblical text for our guidance here: "I would rather be a doorkeeper in the house of my God than dwell in the tents of wickedness" (Ps. 84:10). How many ushers realize that they are doorkeepers in the house of God? And how many of them understand that the doorkeeper is the connecting link between the world and the altar? I tell you that ushers have been important fellows for a long time. I have known a few of the great ones, and men and women by the thousands will rise up and call them blessed.

29. Superiority

In this age of advertising, campaigns are put on to get people to do all kinds of things, even go to church. Most of these periodic attempts to solve spiritual and moral problems by advertising urge you to "Attend the church of your choice." When some churches were bombed in Southern cities because of integration activities, a cartoon admonished people "to bomb the church of your choice." The whole thing made me stop and ask myself what choice has to do with the denomination I call my own.

So far as the majority of us are concerned, I suppose we are still going to the one that we were taken to by our parents. Where we started to Sunday School, we now continue as church members. We would be hard put to say why it is this one rather than another one except that here we are more at home and comfortable. At least, in this one we know something about the nomenclature and the general method of hiring and firing preachers. Along with our political affiliations, we simply grew into our religious affiliations.

Now and then somebody has a quarrel with somebody in the church or violently dislikes the minister and decides he will change his denomination. A few churches in towns where I have lived were made up almost entirely of malcontents. They had grown angry at somebody, somewhere, then simply moved to this church as being the kind of fellowship they thought might fit their likes and dislikes. Sometimes that works out fairly well, but usually if you talk to a few of these people, they still have memories of their former church and they suffer from a church nostalgia.

I have no doubt that there are some who choose a church because of the social class it represents. A friend of mine used to say that a Presbyterian is just a Methodist who made some good investments. One of my good friends, a bishop of the Episcopal Church, prefers to say that Episcopalians were Methodists who had gone to college. There is a little truth in all this because we tend to gravitate toward that center where our own kind of people will be encountered.

Years ago when I was in seminary I was talking with one of my professors about changing denominations, and I have never forgotten his reaction. He said a man could change if he wanted to, but he would discover that churches are pretty much the same everywhere and it really is not worth it. For every problem the new fellowship seems to solve, you will find a couple of new ones not found in the old one. It was rather cynical, but I think now it was a fairly accurate estimate.

After some observation I have come to the conclusion that the church of your choice better not be the one that seems the most comfortable. Maybe that disturbing feeling that keeps the Sunday morning from being an hour's retreat from reality is just what God wants you to experience. Perhaps our text ought to be the one about setting our hand to the plow and not looking back. Stay with it, brethren, and out of it will come joy and health.

30. Hypocrites

Every once in awhile somebody proclaims that he is not going to join the church because there are too many hypocrites in it. I always want to say to him, "My brother, of course there are hypocrites in it as there ought to be." In the eighteenth century a French philosopher proclaimed, "Alas, there are no more hypocrites." He meant, I suppose, that nobody cared about standards of any kind and so felt no need to make some pretense of living up to them. So the word for these self-righteous critics is: "Yes, there are hypocrites in the church, but there is always room for one more. So why don't you come in and join them?"

For the truth is that all of us are hypocrites. We often try to give the impression of being better or worse than we are. I do not get very worried about that unless a fellow starts bragging about it. In that case, just let him alone and he will soon appear so ridiculous in the eyes of all who know him that his neighbors and friends will put him in his proper place.

But with every passing year of my life I am increasingly impressed that more hypocrites can be found per square inch in other organizations than I can find per square yard in the church. Take the opera, for example. How many of the people who go to that operatic production are there because their wives or their friends dragged them to it when they would rather be playing pinochle with the boys? How many go to the opera just to be seen and to wear beautiful clothes? And how few of that crowd do you suppose are there because they love music?

Or what about service clubs? I listen to the high goals they hold up and their proclamation of service above self, and then I see how some of those fellows operate in business. Still I am not a member of a service club today not because I am too good or because there are too many hypocrites in it. But there are plenty of them there.

Hypocrisy is a kind of professional risk for anybody who wants to make something of himself. The church member is at least trying to bring his life under the searching light of God "unto whom all hearts are open, all desires known." And if the preacher is worth his salt, he will hold them all, including himself especially, under the judgment of God.

We are covered with the veneer of pretense. Let a man think back honestly over the events of the day and he will be shocked at the number of things he said and he did not mean. He will be upset with the times he pretended to be something he was not. Then let him take hope from the grace that has brought him to the church. For if he never gets cured completely in that environment, he will never get so proud that he is not gladly numbered one of them.

VI. PREACHING

31. Preachers

Now this book is for laymen and not for preachers, but you must allow me the privilege of saying a word about preachers to laymen. For this is a subject of which there is much ignorance and of which there is much misunderstanding. Most of the fault, I suspect, is the preacher's, but he does not mean it.

Laymen think that the preacher is a special kind of fellow with a certain piosity of spirit that sets him apart from life. You would be surprised to learn that the preacher is usually a fellow who came up out of the same background you came from, and his experience has been about the same as yours. Sometimes he came from a good home and sometimes he did not. He may have belonged to polite society, but often he came from the wrong side of the track. The early home of one of my preachers was back of a bar on the ocean front, and his father and mother were barkeepers.

Preachers like everybody else have a sense of humor, most of them, and they are as tired of the stilted, moralistic air you put on as you are tired of putting it on. It would be a good thing if the congregation could sit in the wings when preachers gather together Sunday evening after the work of the week is ended and they are at rest for about eighteen hours. You will hear more good stories than you would hear at a traveling salesmen's convention, and you would feel more of the sheer joy of being alive than you do watching the laugh-in programs on television.

Some of the preachers are very smart and some are not. Men

in the ministry sometimes have the highest I.Q.'s, and sometimes they are more or less mediocre. But all of them had come to a point where they wanted to make their lives count for the most and were persuaded by God that they could do so in the service of the church.

Most all preachers are hard workers, and they are sincere in wanting to be of service to their people. You should get to know them and become their friends, for oftentimes they are lonely men. Your friendship will mean much to them, and I think theirs will mean much to you.

The hardest thing for a layman to believe is that his minister may be a bashful sort of fellow. Bashful! Why, he stands before a crowd or at least a congregation one or more times a week and talks. He must be ready at the drop of a hat to pray in public or give some appropriate remarks. That guy, thinks the layman, must have a cast-iron nerve. My brother, hear me out.

If you knew how often it takes almost more courage than he can muster for a young preacher to call on a man or a family, you would be surprised. He rings the bell and prays silently that nobody is home. He leaves his card and runs for his car. He is expected to call on the successful business or professional member of his church, and what shall he say to him? Some of you know the answer to that question, but he does not know you and you scare him.

If there is a man in the church who needs a friend, he is that fellow in the pulpit. Protestants believe in the "priesthood of all believers." That does not mean that every vagrant theological idea that comes to you out of your ignorance is to be proclaimed with the same assurance that you give answers to your office boy. But it means that your ministry is a real one and often is to be extended to your minister as a fellow human being who is also finding the going hard. Stop expecting him to be God and welcome him as a fellow pilgrim for whom the road seems to wind uphill all the way.

32. Communication

If there is one part of the church's work that seems quite out-side the laymen's responsibility, it is preaching. They must do what they can through the polity of the church in which they work to get the best preacher possible, and that seems to be an end of their influence or responsibility. Believe me, there is nothing further from the truth, and I speak as an old hand after having preached in all kinds of pulpits and in all kinds of churches over a period of more than twenty years.

The laymen are in some ways the key to the whole business.

Whenever I go to a strange church to preach I can tell almost immediately whether anything important is going on there and whether or not they are having a row. In the case of a split congregation, there is a coldness and a suspicion on the part of people in the pews that is like giving the preacher a cold shower. They do not love their neighbors and there is a kind of hard suspicion in their eyes and attitudes that makes the preaching of the gospel of love almost impossible. A fellow starts to talk and it is like throwing pebbles up against a glass. They bounce back at him, though he struggles along and does the best he can to kindle some faint glow of Christian fellowship. But it is a sorry situation from beginning to end.

On the other hand, if one goes into the pulpit of a church where the congregation is working together in harmony, the preached word seems to head toward the target like a bumble bee aiming for a flower. The sermon has meaning and purpose, and the whole process speaks of a communion of the saints and the presence of the Holy Spirit.

The influence of the laity is always paramount and especially so for a young preacher. How many young men starting out in the ministry have received their vision of what they ought to be by the way their congregation responds to them and deals with them? Preaching belongs to the whole church, and while one man is called to do the actual speaking, preaching is an act of the whole church in which every member participates.

The deaf mute who attended church regularly because he wanted "people to know which side he was on" had a point. But this I speak of is much more than that. It is not simply filling a seat. It is not blowing up the statistics. It is kindling the flame which lightens our way to God.

Laymen, if the preaching in your church leaves much to be desired, make it better.

33. Listening

One of the greatest failures of the ministry is its inability to listen. When he is called upon to speak on so many occasions, the minister, if he is not careful, falls into the habit of meeting every situation with an open mouth. Then when some man in need of counsel calls on him, he is giving him advice long before the poor fellow has had a chance to stumble through his story.

Consider if you will that the layman ministers to the preacher by being a good listener. I will give you an example.

In one of my churches there was a farmer who attended regularly with his family. One day he had come to town on business and dropped by my study. I saw him reluctantly, for I was busy. But he raised a point I had made the previous Sunday and said that as he had been driving his tractor up and down the fields that week, he had begun to think about it. He said to me, "Do you suppose that if you took that idea a little further it might mean this?" And then he came up with something which was central and true and I had missed it. He did not stay very long and soon left me to less important issues.

After that from time to time he would come in and see me. Always he stayed for just a few moments and always with an idea from my sermon that had struck him while he was working on the farm. Always it was to the point and always it stimulated my own mind. Yet, this man had only an eighth grade education, but his mind was always reaching out eagerly for ideas and exploring beyond where the preacher stopped.

This layman and his family were nearly always at church. But when now and then for some reason they were absent, it was always a poorer Sunday for me. There were some professors and Ph.D.'s in my congregation, but somehow it was to this man I turned with a sense of greatest obligation. As I went into the pulpit I would find myself praying, "Lord, help me not to say anything that will sound stupid to Davis when he is riding his tractor this week." And when he was there in the service, he was the one I saw most often as I tried to explore some of the mysteries and proclaim some of the riches of the gospel.

I do not think that the man ever knew what a contribution he made to the preaching in his church. I did try to tell him one time how I felt about it, but in his modesty he was sure I was exaggerating. What makes a great preacher? Well, a good many things go into it. But, believe me, one of the essential things is a great congregation.

34. Clearness

Arrogance is a most unlovely quality in any man and never more so than when it appears in an individual who assumes more knowledge than he possesses. A healthy and humble respect for the other fellow's job and the way he does it is always in order. Some of the foolish things that irritate us the most will turn out to be reasonable procedures when we know the whole story. As a church administrator one of my burdens is to read letters that come from very well-meaning laymen, giving me the answers to complicated problems I have been dealing with for years. I can hardly bear to answer the letters with their naïve proposals. Yet, they spring from well-intentioned individuals oftentimes who sincerely wish that the church were more efficient, more practical, and more helpful.

There is one area, however, where the layman can really help the preacher. Let him do it in the spirit of love, but by all means, let him do it one way or another. I speak of the vocabulary and the form of the minister's preaching. If it is not getting to you and if you have only a vague idea of what is being said, then, by all means, it is your duty to sit down with this brother in Christ and try to help him talk plainly. For preaching is to be heard and understood, not by experts in some particular field, but by all men and that includes you and me.

Probably a kind of discussion group or dialogue is in order. I never knew a minister who wouldn't gladly sit down with some laymen and talk about anything if they requested it. Then as kindly as it can be done, you should point out that what he is saying is put into a vocabulary nobody understands. Probably if you ask him to define some of the words he uses in his discourse, he will have to confess he does not understand exactly what they mean either.

The great men in all fields have had the gift of speaking their truth so simply and directly that laymen can understand them. T. H. Huxley could do it for science, and the theologian if he is worth anything at all learns to do it for religion. I can think of no better treatment for obscure speaking than for a man's loyal friends to take the time to explore the reasons for the obscurity. Plain words, short sentences, the cutting of excessive detail, will all come out as milestones along the path of plain speech.

John Wesley went through his sermons with an intelligent maid who worked for the family, and when she failed to understand a word, he found a simpler one. This is not talking down to the people, but it is developing the great art of plain speech.

A man's wife should do this for him and this is a part of her marital duty. But a man's wife will not always be heard gladly, while a man's parishioner may be listened to if the man has any hope in him at all. Perhaps you can meet occasionally with the preacher and say to him, "My brother, I know that you are a good man. I know that you are talking about something vaguely religious, but I leave this service time after time without the foggiest notion of what you were really trying to say. Now let us reason together from time to time and see if together we cannot get this good news into such form that it can be understood by the sinners." Who knows, you may save a gabbing windbag who may be born again into a spokesman of the Lord, using some plain and lucid prose.

35. Simplicity

One of my laymen called me up a while back and said he was taking a famous philosopher-theologian-scientist to lunch and wondered if I would like to go along. I had read the books of this man for many years and welcomed the chance to meet him. I found him all that I expected and listened to his conversation enthralled. He seemed to know everything about everything—not in the obnoxious sense of that wise guy down the block—but because he is a great scholar and has an exceptional mind. I asked a question now and then to show that I was a college graduate, but I added mighty little to the conversation.

After the lunch as my layman was driving me back to my office, he asked, "Did you understand what he was talking about?" "Well," I replied cautiously, "not all of it." Said my friend, "I understood hardly any of it. I guess I shall just have to be content with the simple teachings of Jesus."

That remark has haunted my mind ever since. Was Jesus simple? Is our Christianity for children? Do the high I.Q.'s and the graduate students discover truth which poor ordinary fellows can neither understand nor possess? "The simple teachings of Jesus" which common men have been hearing gladly for about two thousand years is a far cry from the philosophers and the theologians. But are they inferior?

I make a few general observations:

1. A great many of the profundities which come to us dressed

up in the jargon of the scholars are academic cover-ups for windy clichés.

2. Some speakers want to impress people with their learning, and they do it with big words and obscure language constructions.

3. When a fellow cannot say it plainly, it usually means that his own mind is a bit foggy.

4. The great truths necessary for life are basically simple truths which plain men can comprehend.

5. Jesus speaks in simple terms, but his thoughts are deeper than the sea and higher than the heavens.

Some fellow is always coming along to impress us with himself and to claim a special insight or revelation. Such men tried it in the first century, and the twentieth century has more than its share of them. Sometimes they succeed in frightening the humble and impressing the ignorant. But the church, an old-timer in dealing with phonies, labels them as proud heretics and leads us back to the feet of our Lord.

This is Biblical. Isaiah writes:

> And a highway shall be there,
> and it shall be called the Holy Way;
> the unclean shall not pass over it,
> and fools shall not err therein.
>
> (35:8)

That seems plain enough.

Jesus says:

> I thank thee, Father, Lord of heaven and earth, that thou hast hidden these things from the wise and understanding, and revealed them to babes. . . .
>
> (Matt. 11:25)

Brethren, those simple teachings of Jesus take a man right to the heart of the truth about life and man and God. Do not be scared off by the learned windbags.

36. Tolerance

A cartoon is sometimes better than a sermon, and week after week it is hard to surpass *The New Yorker* in this department. Some time ago one of their artists showed the front of a church with the congregation coming out after the service. Everybody is fighting with everybody else, and one lady is hitting the minister over the head with an umbrella. A man and his wife passing by on the street observe the conflict and she says to him, "Goodness, what do you suppose the rector's message for the troubled world was this time?"

I suspect that many a layman leaves his church feeling that this scene represents the way he feels and the way a good many of his brethren feel. They came to the house of God for comfort, and they received irritation. They were seeking the green pastures and the quiet streams, and they were hurled into a pitched battle where they have been all week. A man comes to the conclusion that whatever else he does not need it is certainly not more argument and more bitterness and more frustration.

Well, let it be said at once that the layman has a real point. But I would if I could speak a word for the poor preacher. He has to make the gospel relevant, and by no stretch of the imagination can it be said that our Lord counseled us to regard his way as a retreat. There are great issues at stake and Christians have to be involved. The idea that the church is a hospital or a rest home is not to be found anywhere in the Scriptures. That is why people who want that kind of religion have to find it somewhere outside Christianity.

Yet the layman has a real point and Sunday ought to be a change of pace for him and his family. But if the preacher is not taking the great conflicts of life and putting them in their eternal setting, he is not doing his job properly. We are not to come out of church wanting to fight one another or fight the preacher because we disagree with his ideas. We ought to come out of church with a sense that this is not an easy life we are living and that there are very great issues at stake. But we ought to feel that we have caught at least a glimpse of God's ultimate purpose and that His Kingdom is our goal. This demands sacrifice and hard work, and our fellowship is with our fellow Christians who may not see it quite the way we see it but who are committed to the same goal just as we are.

Fights in churches are nearly always over minor matters. Indeed, when somebody tries to define what his source of irritation is, it usually sounds so petty that even he is ashamed of it when he has tried to get it into words. This is what we must avoid at all costs.

If the layman can find grace to say to himself that the one with whom he disagrees really wants about the same thing that he does, that is a good start. Let no chasm be dug between the right and the left or between the conservative and the liberal. Indeed, let us keep bright our own convictions as we polish them on the abrasive surface of other personalities. And, above all, have a little talk with the preacher before you write him off. You may discover he is after something you too think is important, only he did not say it very well on that particular occasion.

VII. THEOLOGY

37. Trinity

A layman gets very tired of some of the abstractions that pass for religious truth. And so do I. We are the products of a practical civilization, and we are citizens of a nation that has succeeded by emphasizing practical results.

The doctrine that falls first under our antagonism is the Trinity. Who can talk about one God and at the same time talk about three persons? This is the kind of double talk, or triple talk, that a man has little patience with, and he can raise little enthusiasm for it.

It is not only the laymen but sometimes our modern preachers who want to discard the whole business of the Trinity and forget it. There was even a bishop of a perfectly orthodox church who made another headline by attacking this doctrine.

I think it was Reinhold Niebuhr, one of the leading Christian thinkers of our time, who said that a doctrine is to be judged not only by what it says but by what happens when we deny it. This made an impression on me, and I think there is no better example of what he may have had in mind than this doctrine of the Trinity. Suppose you don't like it; suppose it does not seem logical; suppose it seems to be unnecessarily mysterious and esoteric? Ah, but what happens when it is eliminated?

Fortunately for us, there are examples of what happens when churches believe that the Trinity is outmoded and never was essential. They find difficulty in maintaining a belief in God, and sometimes go so far as to put humanity in the place of deity. They are always in danger of ending up in believing that Jesus was a good man and a good teacher all right, but have lost all recognition of his redeeming power. They can become an ethical society, but have great difficulty in maintaining their status as a religion.

The doctrine of the Trinity, my friends, is oftentimes stated too baldly and too literally. We should never talk about "three persons." What it was trying to make clear when it was first enunciated was that God is transcendent and God is also immanent. The doctrine wanted to be sure we did not forget that God was in Christ reconciling the world to Himself.

My advice would be to see it as a check against an extreme humanism and against an extreme transcendentalism. Do not throw it out, but marvel at the wisdom of our fathers who gave us an anchor to a central truth of faith. And do not worry about the impossibility of ever making it as logical as a mathematical proposition. We do not know how to explain a drop of water.

38. Authority

Practically all the laymen I know respect experience and authority in most fields. They are in the habit of dealing with salesmen who know more about the product than they know, and so they ask questions and listen attentively to the answers. They are aware that it is foolishness to embark upon some economic adventure without getting expert advice. They may not like the fellow personally, but if his training and experience are such that he obviously knows more about the subject than they know, they will listen to him even if he does not use the proper mouthwash and has never heard about deodorants. Getting the facts is more important than approving or disapproving the salesman's personality.

But the same fellow in a church is likely to assume that he knows more about theology than the preacher. He will feel that especially if he does not like the preacher and can criticize some of his personal habits. Yet, practically all churches have as their leaders men who have spent anywhere from three to six years in graduate study. They have been subjected to biblical study which gives them an understanding of the latest opinions of the scholars, and they know about the Dead Sea Scrolls. It would seem that they must have something to say that might be worth hearing because they have been students of religion.

Why is it that so many laymen assume that in religion everybody is an expert? Why is it that a layman dared to say to me arrogantly that he knew much more about the Bible than his preacher? And of course he did not hesitate to tell him so. Why is it that in this mysterious and awesome business of trying to apprehend who God is and what He is about, we take the attitude that ignorance is an advantage?

I propose to my lay brethren a radical point of view. Why not assume for the time being that the minister is a fellow who knows some things that are essential to life here and to life in the hereafter? Why not assume for the moment, at least, that if he does not say it too well and can sometimes say it in a way that makes you angry, still you had better weigh his words and consider them objectively? Why not put some of the emphasis on this rather than on whether or not he is a nice fellow with a pleasing manner? Surely, the thoughtful layman in our time is not going to prefer the shallow man with the salesman personality over the serious man whose studies can uncover deep truths if we have the patience to hear him gladly.

The preacher, brethren, is really an expert in some fields. When you are listening to an expert and you know that he knows more about some of these things than you do, would it not be sensible to pick his brains and see if something of his spirit may not overflow on you? It may not always add to your enjoyment to take this point of view, but it surely will increase your knowledge. And maybe it will give the essential clue you have been seeking. Remember that St. Paul said the treasure was in earthen vessels.

39. Miracle

The Old Testament tells the great story of Moses who killed an Egyptian overseer and then fled to the desert for safety. There he settled down for a time to look after his father-in-law's sheep. But one day he heard the voice of God speaking to him out of a burning bush that "burned with fire, and the bush was not consumed" (Exod. 3:2, AV). A naturalist who has made a special study of the land of the Bible says that the bush might have been a thorny acacia in which a crimson mistletoe grows. At certain times of the year the flame-colored flowers of the mistletoe make the shrub seem to blaze with fire when seen from a distance. Do you suppose that is what Moses saw when he had that great experience? There was a time when I would have been very disturbed by this possibility. Today I hope this is the explanation and I'll tell you why.

It would mean that God uses ordinary things through which to reveal Himself. Indeed, the story of the Bible and His revelation is a testimony of how the Almighty appears to men in ordinary affairs if they are ready to see Him. It is good news that out of a desert shrub covered with a mistletoe parasite, the "flaming bush" got the attention of Moses and he heard a divine call to duty and to greatness.

One of the worst mistakes we make in our time is to assume that if a thing is to be religious, it has to be miraculous. If we can understand it, then obviously it is in the realm of science and not of religion. This was never true in the Bible. Those people assumed that all the world is a miracle and that God reveals Himself in the daily affairs and in the ordinary occurrences.

If this is true, as I believe it is, then Christians must be ready to take off their shoes because the ground is holy at any time and in every place. The revelation of God comes through office affairs as well as in the sanctuary. It meets us on Main Street during the noon hour as well as on some high mountain in the springtime. If this is an unreligious age, as I suppose it is, the reason is not an absence of God but an absence of sensitivity on our part to His presence.

When we actually begin to understand the construction of the ordinary growing things, we see miracles. And when we are aware of the wonder of human relationship, there appears to our souls the great God who made us "and not we ourselves." The difference between the biblical world and us is that their eyes had not been blinded by sophistication and a loss of the sense of the mysterious. They could still see. Lord, open our eyes!

40. Creed

I was brought up on the Apostles' Creed, and no service seems quite adequate unless we repeat it. But we do not use it many places anymore, and some of the younger preachers would rather be caught dead than repeating this old, out-of-date affirmation of faith.

I am perfectly willing to agree that some of the phrases need to be interpreted in modern terms, but when a congregation knows what was being said, what affirmations were being proclaimed, and what heresies denied, it will not have much trouble with the Apostles' Creed. All church members need some help in this field, and that is one thing preachers are for.

But consider one very significant point. The new creeds for the most part deal with philosophical concepts. They deal with general propositions about God and about the world. In this main characteristic they show how far the modern church has gone from real religion into the field of philosophy.

Read the Apostles' Creed and notice that it is concerned primarily with reciting the great acts of God. It tells us what God did rather than describe the attributes of Deity. It is historically centered and refers to Pontius Pilate's time as that of the Crucifixion and the Resurrection. Repeat it again and discover how it is concerned to say what Jesus Christ did and how he was the action of God.

This is our faith and this is the Christian religion. It is ever aware of a God who acts in history. And while some theologians will write long books on the nature of God and His world, the Bible is mostly concerned to tell us what God has been doing.

Christianity is something anchored in the actions of God rather than something you philosophize about. It is a happening on the streets of time rather than an idea to meditate on in cloister or in the study. The early Christians were called the followers of the Way and never thought of themselves as scholars set apart to study the characteristics of the Almighty. Christians are those who are where the action is because it is God's action which is all-important.

Perhaps you begin to see why I like the Apostles' Creed. I like to repeat in the service the words about the Author of my faith and the Maker of heaven and earth and the One who was crucified, dead and buried, and then rose again. I like all those active verbs that tell me that I worship not an "unmoved mover" but that the Father of men calls me to join Him in realizing the new Kingdom. Every time you substitute contemplation for action, you have missed the point.

Modern men spend time and much ink defining and analyzing what we mean by truth. The Fourth Gospel puts down Jesus' word: "I am the truth." The New Testament simply assumes that truth is personal and for us, that it is something we *do*. The Apostles' Creed has not lost this request for action. Unfortunately, we have.

41. Theology

This is a time when the intellectuals in the church demand a theology for everything they do. The layman is likely to get restless and nervous under this barrage because theology spells for him dry-as-dust talk and pious terms thrown around to cover ignorance. In his business it is quite obvious that he has to do certain things and deal with certain problems. Nobody ever suggests he must first of all spell out a philosophical justification for paying the rent or selling the product.

But in the church we cannot be satisfied with the simple proposition that we need the money and that most people are not giving enough. We cannot even be content with a straight tithing proposition that we owe at least 10 per cent of our income to the church and related good causes. We must have a "theology of stewardship" which by the time it is discussed and organized has grown academic and unreal. Any impulse we might have felt to open our purses a little wider and be shamed by our niggardly giving, has disappeared, and we are content to drowse away while the brethren discuss the theology.

It is not enough to say that if you have experienced the Christian faith in such a way that it has changed your life, you must tell other people about it. You must have a "theology of evangelism." This takes a good deal of time to set forth and a good many words to define and analyze. The inner glow of happiness fades away. While the theology is being produced, the energy we could have spent telling our neighbor about the Lord is spent going to classes and hearing dull words about dull propositions.

All of this comes about because we have the thing wrong end to. We think we must just sit down and spell out reasons and orthodox arguments for some action. Rather, we should let the impulse touch us and move us and then later on spell out its meaning from the experience. The very word "theology" simply means thinking about God, and this always implies experience. If you haven't done anything and haven't felt anything, then you haven't anything to write about or lecture about anyway.

Some people still believe that the first-century Christians read the letters of St. Paul and the Gospels in a seminar and then went about founding the church and evangelizing the world. But those early Christians did not have any New Testament, they merely wrote it. The wonder of it all is that when Christians heard, believed, and went to work, the New Testament came up out of their life and experience. Did you ever notice how much of the New Testament is testimony about what the Lord was doing for the world through the followers of Christ?

Next time the inner voice commands you to say something or do something for someone else in the name of Christ, you do it and then tell somebody what happened to them and to you. That, my brother, will be theology.

42. Smallness

A man went to work for a Volkswagen agency. He was shown around the plant and the product explained to him. As the manager turned away, he said to him, "And remember, if I catch you thinking big, you're fired." That may be all right for Volkswagens, but we think that religion has to do with thinking big thoughts and catching big visions. Our main emphasis is on the expanding horizon and the profound insights. But maybe this Volkswagen fellow had a point and Christians spend too much time thinking big and ought to begin thinking small.

It is hard for us to believe that God is present in ordinary affairs. We look for the mysterious and the inexplicable. Indeed, for many of us He is the "God of the gaps." Religion, we assume, begins when we enter the misty and the obscure. If a scientist or a mathematician can give us a logical answer as to why something works the way it does, we assume immediately that this belongs now to science, and religion must look elsewhere for its material. Indeed, we interpret past generations as religious precisely because of their ignorance. It was a religious time because it did not know the answer to its problems.

How about a new look at this matter and a new approach? What if God leads us on the path to discovery and finds that He has had a good day when suddenly a flash of insight on the part of some man reveals the mystery? What if God thinks that this is His main work and that a man should feel he is never closer to the Divine than when he gets a clue to the explanation of the unknown?

If God belongs only in the gaps, then of course we must expect God to be pushed out of more and more of our life. For the truth is that man keeps on closing the gaps with his knowledge, and this process which has speeded up in our time probably will go faster as time goes on. This may be what some of the theological brethren have in mind when they talk about Dietrich Bonhoeffer's phrase, "Man come of age." Personally, I have never been impressed that the condition of our world shows that man has yet shown any real ability in managing either things or himself.

Let us back up on this and think of God in daily life and in the family. Let us stop looking so far away and look close at home. In a word, let us follow the Volkswagen man's admonition and see God's presence in the small, the unassuming, and the everyday. My guess is that it will bring us closer to the biblical world, and that would be a mighty good thing for us. Quit looking so far away that you stumble over the revelation at your feet.

VIII. WAY

43. Professional

The fellow that caused me the greatest trouble as a preacher was the Conference Lay Leader. He was the man chosen to represent laymen in the councils of the church. For some reason he was always antagonistic to the ministry of the church. Whether this was because I had not shown him the proper deference or because I did not open the pulpit to him on Laymen's Day, I do not know.

Since that time I have met a number of these brethren whom I would call the "professional" laymen. They usually appear at the head table when the bishop is present. They make the speeches when you want a leading layman on the program. They serve on the boards when you want the laity represented. They are either retired men or they have some job that will let them loose any time they need to appear. They have really made a profession out of being laymen and they are very impressive, until one sees what they are doing in their local church.

I remember one layman who was always talking about tithing with the implication, of course, that his gifts to the church causes were astronomical. I followed up on this one and tried to find out where his 10 per cent was going. I never found a single agency within the church receiving a nickel from him. I even did the sneaky thing of inquiring at his local church and found that his annual gifts were less than some of the working girls were contributing. I could not prove it, but I think he was lying when he talked about giving to the church. I have a sneaky kind of mind.

I knew another fellow who had finally established himself on this professional laymen's circuit, who was nothing but trouble for every minister where he attended church. Not only that, but he refused to stay by whenever he disagreed with the message from the pulpit. You always had to ask where his membership was now because he may have had a row the previous week and walked out to another church.

Of course, these are rare specimens and only common enough to give articulate itinerant laymen a bad name. Their trouble, I suspect, arises out of a frustrated ambition to be a member of the professional staff. That is a legitimate ambition if the Lord has called you to preach. But there is no higher calling in the Kingdom than to be a Christian doctor, a Christian lawyer, or a Christian businessman whose whole professional career is laid at the feet of Christ. When these men speak, everybody listens, including the local congregation. When I am in their presence, I know what the Creed means when it speaks about "the communion of saints."

But may the good Lord deliver us from the professional boys whose words are only impressive when they are far from home.

44. Happiness

Wisdom often appears to us these days either on bulletin boards or on automobile bumper strips. One of the gems observed recently on a car just ahead of me on the Freeway proclaimed: "War is hell. But then so is peace." You will be hard put to find a more pessimistic outlook than those words reflect. Was the fellow who dreamed that up sick? Or was he just on the edge of suicide?

Probably the truth is that he was neither, that he was reflecting on what thoughtful men discover about themselves and life soon or late. A particular outward circumstance may help us for the time being, but so far as solving the problems of life is concerned, it never quite brings it off. Peace is certainly preferable to war. But if anybody thinks that peace means an ideal life for all the citizens, let him think again. The truth is that there are men, and I have talked with them, who look back upon the war with nostalgia. It was the one time when they seemed to know what they were doing and why they were doing it. It was the one time when life had some particular purpose they believed in and all their energies were devoted to it. Incidentally, it was the one time when they were far from the responsibilities of civilian life, their only worries being orders and staying alive.

Strangely enough, it is the gospel that brings us this insight that peace can be hell as well as war. For the gospel never promises men that they will find happiness no matter what their outward circumstances may be. The fellow who thinks that life has promised him a right to be happy never read his Bible. Life makes no such promise to us.

But what the gospel gives us is a sense of adventure. Life is satisfactory to us only when it has some meaning which we are pursuing and in which we believe. This is the essential thing. What Christianity does is to bring us to Christ who gives us a vision for ourselves and our world from the perspective of God.

The final security it affords us is the realization that what happens to us on the outside is not so important as what kind of people we are on the inside. The only assurance I can have that I will come through the crisis, the tragedy, the failure which are part of the human lot, is the assurance of a strength not my own which is given to him who trusts in his Lord.

This sets us free from a lot of nonsense, a lot of false expectation, and makes us less envious of what some people seem to have which has been denied us. It fills our minds with a certain honest cynicism about the promises of the world, and it creates a distrust of treasures on earth. But with that healthy cynicism there comes to us also a deep faith that the way we feel depends primarily on the way we are.

The Christian is set free because he knows that both war and peace can be hell and that heaven is God's gift to His heart through Christ.

45. Dominion

I got into a conversation the other day with a man about the new superjets which are supposed to be just around the corner. I took a dim view toward them and their implication, but he was of the opinion that we have no choice. He said that if we did not build them other nations would get ahead of us and that in any case these jumbos with their speed faster than sound meant progress. By the tone of his voice I felt that I should have taken off my hat and bowed my head.

I have been thinking about this ever since that conversation. I know a good many people for whom bringing these screeching monsters into our cities already too full of noise and confusion is the furthest thing from what they desire. I know people who think that we are going fast enough and that there is not much to be gained by going to New York in one hour instead of five. But there seems to be a curious obeisance paid to whatever science says is possible, as if that meant that now it has to be done.

Do you suppose that man is despondent because he no longer controls his life? What was that good word in Genesis? "Be fruitful and multiply, and fill the earth and subdue it; and have dominion over the fish of the sea and over the birds of the air and over every living thing that moves upon the earth" (1:28). Now suddenly we are no longer to have dominion over the earth, but progress, whatever we may mean by that, has dominion over us.

The restoration of human confidence is a religious thing. My recovery from an unspoken but ever-present despair is to bring myself back to God. And while this is so naïve as to seem shocking to some of you, it can only be worship which will restore our sense of dominion over life precisely because we are the children of God.

Think about this next Sunday morning while the offering is being taken. Remind yourself that only the church is committed to this point of view and supports the proclamation of this message. What would life really be without it?

You see, what the church is always concerned about is human beings. It believes that nothing is any good unless men are served. It believes that all the improvements we make, and they are mighty and impressive, are in vain unless human life becomes richer and filled with a deeper joy. This is what the choir is singing about and this is what the preacher is praying and preaching about. The church believes that unless people come together and think about God and worship Him, they will lose their way and worship such idols as Progress.

The church has not persisted longer than any other institution because it puts on the best show once a week. It does not endure because it is tops in the entertainment field. It does not command loyalty because its personnel is more talented or brighter than in any other organization. It continues because it always reminds people who they are and warns against forces which will make them forget.

The one unchanging note that sounds through the church's speech and actions is that man made in the image of God will be finished whenever he yields his dominion over things and worships them. And if you will look around, even hastily, you will see too many people who no longer have dominion over anything, not even themselves. Some of them are your neighbors and your friends. There is nothing like an hour a week in church to restore a fellow's mind to a proper perspective.

46. Triumph

Sometimes when I am in church, the service gets off on such a low note that I never recover my confidence. You know how it is. Starts are so important that a bad one kills a fellow's expectancy.

The kind of thing I am referring to usually has a call to worship in a subdued mood, as if it were time for bed and mother is calming her child with a lullaby. It is often "good" music and like as not somebody such as Beethoven or Brahms wrote it. The music experts, of which I am not one, think it is great and close their eyes in bliss.

Then the choir starts down the aisle to the opening hymn. The hymn chosen would be excellent for a wake, and the choir members stroll along as if they were members of the bereaved family. They do not march; they meander. By this time I am getting drowsy and it is hard to cover up the yawns.

The minister gets into the spirit of the thing and gives forth with an invocation that is gentle and no more invigorating than the hum of bees in summer. Everything is so well-mannered and genteel that I hope they never find out what I am thinking.

But once in awhile I am in a service that is quite different and wonderful. The call to worship sounds like trumpets, not violins. One I remember with joy gave us the opening line of "A Mighty Fortress Is Our God." Great! The processional hymn was four/four time and full of affirmations about God's majesty and power. The choir members marched as if they were going somewhere and they did not have all day to get there. Wonderful!

The preacher reminded us who we were and what we were gathered together to proclaim. He spoke strongly of the greatness of our God and the majesty of the Church of Christ. I tell you I could hardly wait for the next thing to happen, and drowsing or yawning was so far from me that I was invigorated and felt like saying Hallelujah.

Now this is the way a Christian service of worship ought to start and continue, for this is the way of the Christian faith. We are not called by our Lord to rest and retreat but to joy and life. We do not gather in the church to drone through prayers and hymns but to hear a bugle. Our mood should be that of a baseball or football crowd's when the trumpet rings out and they yell "Charge!" For weariness is not cured by boredom but by inspiration.

The artist Burne-Jones attended the funeral service of his friend Robert Browning. He was not pleased with it and said: "Much would I have given for a banner or two, and much would I have given had a chorister come out of the triforium and rent the air with a trumpet." He had the sure sense of what a Christian's funeral should be.

If we are triumphant in death, then surely we should be triumphant in life. Indeed, the New Testament almost shocks us with its emphasis on rejoicing in the midst of trouble. Jesus Christ wreaks havoc on all our moods of despair and defeat. When Christians gather for their worship on Sunday, the mood must be yes.

These words are for the music committee primarily. Do not ask the minister to deal with this problem—I mean this opportunity. But let the brave laymen take their responsibility and help the musicians discard their muted strings and bring out their brass. Especially at the beginning.

47. Revelation

The Crucifixion seems to us to be the pivotal event in all history. To the people living in Jerusalem at that time, I doubt that it seemed important in any way. Crucifixions were common enough in the Roman world. That was the common means of executing criminals and subversive people dangerous to the state. Indeed, Anatole France has a story about Pilate, who had retired from politics and was living in a Mediterranean city. A traveler asked him one time if he remembered a certain Jesus of Nazareth who was crucified when Pilate was the Roman governor in Judea. Pilate thought about it for a moment and finally shook his head. "I do not remember the man," he said.

The great event seldom seemed great at the time it happened. Only after we look backward and see its significance in terms of what came out of it are we able to say that this or that happening was crucial and decisive.

This is one of the great things about the Bible. The things it talks about and the happenings which it relates were not of exceptional importance to anybody outside that small country at the eastern end of the Mediterranean Sea. And even in that small country these things were not important except to a few people who had faith and could see the hand of God in contemporary events. The Bible actually is a book about how God acts through minor characters in small plays.

The Christian layman thinks sometimes that his work is of no importance because he does not think it results in earth-shaking events. A man said to me not long ago that he was only a layman and seemed apologetic in talking to me about something in the church. I said to him that there is no higher calling in the world than to be a Christian layman and that the church has no more important man within it than the layman. Let no one ever apologize because he is not a member of the clergy but is "only a layman."

Actually, the man who speaks a good word, performs a simple Christian act, may not see it at the time but it can be the beginning of something very exciting and very important. Great men often look back to some simple thing that some man said at a particular time that changed their lives. The truth is that the God who made the world and all who dwell in it hardly ever finds important people to reveal Himself through. It is nearly always a rather simple person who becomes to his brethren the incarnation of God.

I would not suggest for a moment that what I do or you do is going to have the effect of the Crucifixion of Christ. But I am going to insist that what you do and what I do may be to some of our brethren the greatest event that ever took place in their experience. If I had the space I could tell you about some Christian men and women in my own life and experience who changed my direction and strengthened my faith. It is the ordinary event which spreads Christian love like a fragrant perfume that becomes the extraordinary revelation of God.

Rise and sing:

> Let the lower lights be burning!
> Send a gleam across the wave!
> Some poor fainting, struggling seaman
> You may rescue, you may save.

48. Wonderful

A man named Russell Maltby was a much loved Methodist figure in Britain a generation or so ago. He was a lawyer and what Methodists call a "local preacher," which is really a layman who preaches the gospel whenever he has a chance and with some regularity. Maltby was a great evangelist and never missed an opportunity to tell the story of the miracle of the gospel. He once had a long talk with a man about the Christian revelation and how God so loved the world that He gave His only begotten son for its redemption. The man said, "Well, I still don't know whether it is true or not that God came down to earth for us men and for our salvation, but I do know that it is the most beautiful thought that ever entered the mind of man." "Then," asked Maltby eagerly, "aren't you prepared to believe that God might think that, too?"

Have you ever stopped to think that if the gospel is true it is the most wonderful and exciting news men ever heard? Preachers sometimes succeed in making the good news dull and monotonous, but that takes real genius. For any man to let this Word enter his mind and possess his imagination will make him see it as news so wonderful that it has to be proclaimed and demonstrated.

This has never been the sole possession of the clergy and, indeed, it is preeminently the possession of plain men who make their living in some other vocation. It is the layman who can best bring this good word to others when the professional clergyman finds that he is regarded with suspicion and distrust.

Maltby was quite right. If this sounds exciting to us and wonderful, could it not be that it must have seemed that way to God? He must have concluded that if men were to understand Him at all, this would be the story that would interpret the mystery. We must not believe that because it seemed simple to us that it is not profound. Surely, the message that the great God came to us through His son is so overpowering that it will destroy all our pride and make all our wisdom appear foolishness. This has been the claim of the gospel from the beginning.

Never let the idea that the church is built on something prosaic and dull take hold of your mind. Make sure always that while some people may not believe it and some will say it is a dangerous idea, none can say it is a bore. Is it not amazing and wonderful that God does not come to us in a theory or a proposition but in the man who was crucified? Once this news gets around we may find ourselves at the center of a new revolution. Amen.

IX. WITNESS

⸙
───
⸙

49. Renewal

In my office we have a Christmas party every year which is not the same kind of thing some of you laymen attend. There is coffee and no liquor; Christmas carols and no stein songs; and the only women involved are wives and secretaries. We exchange gifts which are not to exceed three dollars. You get the picture. Some of you have probably lost interest already. But I tell you we have a good time, and it is one of the affairs during the Christmas season that I always save a place for.

A Christmas or so ago one of the young men in the Treasurer's Office gave me a flashlight for my present. I was grateful for it because you can never have too many of those things. My only problem has been that when I need a flashlight, the batteries are dead. I was saying to this young man some months later than I noticed that the flashlight he gave me was beginning to grow a little dim and I was going to have to buy some new batteries. He told me that if I took off the back part of that flashlight, I would find it could be plugged in and recharged. Sure enough, I took off the end case, plugged it in overnight, and it was as bright as new.

I began to think that something of this kind is what I need and most people I know need. My spiritual life has a tendency to run down and grow dim. It lacks the sharp brightness of real Christianity. It gets to be like too many of the lives I know, and it has no ability to brighten or to guide.

As I thought about this I was reminded of something St. Paul wrote. He said to the Ephesians: ". . . and be renewed in the spirit of your minds . . ." (4:23). Suddenly it seemed to me that the apostle was talking about an experience which would do for a man's life what plugging in that flashlight did for it.

God apparently thought a fellow would need this about once a week, and so He has set aside one day for rest and worship. Not that it cannot happen to us at other times and more often. But we should remember that at least on one day out of seven we must gather in the sanctuary and plug our lives into the Eternal.

What an advantage we Christians have over the poor world-lings who have never developed this habit. They go along day after day doing the same kind of thing, and gradually their spiritual insights grow dim. I do not wonder that we have nervous collapses and moral breaks. But to us there has been shown a secret and a way. The next time I am in the church I am going to think of myself as that flashlight which is constructed so that it can be plugged into the source of power. I am going to believe that God made me like a flashlight. I am going to plug in again with joy and appreciation as I have been doing for many years, and the following week this poor, feeble faith of mine will shine renewed into the darkness. And if I get a little brighter, I will also get a little happier.

50. Retreat

I was reading through the Book of Psalms the other day, which is always a good thing to do, and I came to these words:

> And I say, "O that I had wings like a dove!
> I would fly away and be at rest;
> yea, I would wander afar,
> I would lodge in the wilderness. . . ."
>
> (55:6–7)

As I pondered these poetic words, it came to me that what that writer was saying was simply that he was fed up. He wanted to get out of the city where there were too many people and get out into the wilderness, and he was wishing for wings that would get him there as soon as possible. I said to myself that this is to be expected in this modern world with all its pressure, its crowds, and mechanized life. But how come a man living in an uncomplicated agricultural society in a wide-open simple world of long before the birth of Christ had such a feeling? This was something that belongs to the overworked executive or the man living in the megalopolis who finds it almost impossible to have a moment of quiet or a place that is the least bit private.

I suppose this is what men have always felt when they are overwhelmed with obligations and duties and families and relatives. So that ancient poet speaks words which a man in mid-twentieth century understands. Then I thought of another Old Testament word written by Isaiah. He said:

But they who wait for the Lord shall renew their strength,
they shall mount up with wings like eagles,
they shall run and not be weary,
they shall walk and not faint.

(40:31)

He knew what this feeling is and he had found in his religion strength to wait and the power to mount up to the high places for vision. But, best of all, he had found strength to continue the weary march. In his thinking, this was the climax of the whole business, and to be able to "walk and not faint" is the sure sign of Christian character and Christian witness. The Bible is an old book but it speaks to modern conditions.

We will win it or lose it not according to how high up we can get or how far we can see. The crucial time is when we are so tired we can hardly put one foot in front of the other and we want to quit. That is the time our faith comes in all its wonder and power. Good news!

51. Freedom

I still meet Christian laymen from time to time who get all upset because of something the preacher implied or even said openly. They are afraid that he will upset the faith of other Christians. They seem to assume that his chief task is to make sure that all faithful members of the church never have any doubts sown in their minds nor any questions raised concerning the faith once delivered to the saints. Indeed, their attitude is somewhat like that of the old lady who, upon hearing of the theory of evolution, said, "God grant that it isn't true, but if it is true, God grant that not many people will hear about it."

That kind of religion is not worth very much, and there is more of it around than there ought to be. The man who is always secretly afraid that something is going to be read or discovered that will deny the validity of the propositions he has built his life on, is of all men most miserable. In the secular world they are the men so frightened of the tender nature of democracy that they must not let any communist ever speak openly. They are the men who will not allow nonconformists on the faculties of our universities.

If faith means anything it means confidence and assurance. It is a poor kind of citizen who believes that democracy cannot stand up under the hammer blows of some opposing system. This reactionary protection of an idea or a system is regarded as strength by some of the timid souls, but actually it is a revelation of weakness and fear. The strong believer throws his conviction into the open competition of the market place with confidence that at the end of the day, it has to win.

The man who comes to the conclusion that nothing can disturb his faith in Christianity is set free from many little worries and concerns. It is a miserable experience if one is always suspicious lest some new discovery will destroy his religion. How good it is when we can take seriously the spirit of Jesus' statement in the Fourth Gospel that if we know the truth, the truth shall set us free. How wonderful it is when we conclude that if anything is true, it is of God and therefore it is the Christian's privilege to welcome any new truth.

Let Christian laymen therefore rejoice that in this battering world in which we live they are committed to something so tough and durable that nothing can upset it. It may demand some readjustment of our own beliefs, but that only means that they were partial in the first place and can now be placed on a firmer foundation. This is the free church and the free congregation, and it is the only place for the worship of free men.

52. Gospel

Practically every churchman knows that the word "gospel" means "good news." Yet I do not think there is any obvious thing in our religion that is more generally forgotten than this simple fact. Preachers forget it and give academic discourses full of facts and figures, and sometimes exude great eloquence about everything. But there is no good news in the sermon. So the layman forgets that Christianity is gospel, i.e., good news.

I have known men and so have you, whose understanding of their religion seemed to contain not one whisper about something good and great which God has told them about themselves and their destiny. Christianity becomes a series of duties and obligations with no fun connected with it. It is full of duties but no proclamation of freedom. It is a word about obligations but not a single hint of release. There seems to be in this whole business a great deal about the serious facing of life's problems but nothing about songs in the night and joy unspeakable and full of glory.

Let the church be an organization for the propagation of laughter. And let it be a meeting of kindred minds to kindle goodwill and happiness. In a word, let us get back once again to an understanding of this gospel which has been proclaimed to us and now is to be proclaimed through us to our world. Brethren, it is good news.

Now we may go wrong if we assume that good news always has to be optimistic news. This is where some of our modern religion falls so flat. G. K. Chesterton one time remarked that the gospel is the good news of original sin. He had a point, and it is necessary for us to keep clear in our minds that we believe in something that certainly does not shut its eyes to the tragedy and pain of living. We must not forget that the symbol we go by is the cross which means crucifixion and suffering. But the rejoicing comes when we understand that it was this cross that brought to us the knowledge of the love of God and of His concern for all men forever.

When Samuel Johnson met a man he had known in college thirty years before, the man rejoiced that his old schoolmate was now a famous philosopher. "I once had an ambition to be a philosopher myself," he confided, "but cheerfulness kept breaking in." Christians are those who cannot keep cheerfulness from breaking in. For underneath all that life brings to them and all that they observe in a world that is often sad, there is the whisper that all is well.

It was this experience that gave the early church its power. It may be that its recovery will restore a lost radiance to the modern church. Loosen up and rejoice in the Lord. That is the best theological argument I know.

53. Love

The Green Bay Packers who have taken their place along with the former New York Yankees in baseball and the Boston Celtics in basketball as champions of champions, are always a subject of great interest to sports fans. Coach Lombardi, who resigned in 1968, stands as an example of a man who knows how to mold individual athletes into a great team. He has been tough, and as one of the Packers remarked, "He treats us all the same. Just like dogs." On a national TV show some time ago Lombardi was being interviewed as to his methods and the reasons why he thought the Green Bay Packers were such a success. His answer to this question was a startling one to me when he said they were a success "because they have respect for one another. . . . They have a great deal of love for one another."

I thought of Jesus' teaching that God operates through love and that Christians are those who love one another. Was our Lord thinking of something similar to what Lombardi had said? Can it be true that these tough men who indulge in a kind of legalized mayhem once a week during the season are examples of men loving one another? Is this what the New Testament is all about after all?

Then it came to me that probably this is exactly what the New Testament is saying to us. It was not indulging in some silly romantic idealism about everything being nice if we would just be "loving" to one another. It was talking about life that is tough for everybody and demands toughness of character to endure. It was telling us that when men fight the good fight together and get hurt together, there is born in them that new quality revealed by Jesus Christ. I can imagine that if our Lord walked the earth today and someone should ask him what he thought about Lombardi's statement, he would reply, "Why, of course, that is exactly what I have been telling you. Whatever did you think I meant by love?"

The next time you are thinking about the Bible and the Christian faith, think about the Green Bay Packers as the example we are being told to follow. And when you read the greatest poem about love that was ever written, the 13th chapter of St. Paul's first letter to the Corinthians, do not have in mind the birds and the flowers. But think of that hard, grueling game the Packers and other professional football players indulge in during the autumn of every year.

St. Paul used the gladiatorial games for his illustrations, and what he could have done with professional football! Laymen and martyrs, let us love each other, which is to say, let us fight and struggle for the goals of the Kingdom until we get hurt. Out of that experience, we shall learn at long last what our Lord meant when he told us to love one another. It may not be what we expected. But believe me, it is no flabby idea.

54. Faith

I take a long walk on Saturday when I am home both for the physical exercise as well as the chance to clear my mind. Last winter I came around a sharp bend in the road up in the Hollywood hills and found a little boy resting and looking out across the valley. It was a cloudy day and had been raining. It looked as if it might begin again most any moment. I stopped to visit with him and found him a most interesting youngster. Finally, I said to him, "Son, do you think it's going to rain?" He looked around and replied, "I don't know, but if it does, I 'spect I can find some shelter." As I have thought about that reply, it seems to me that it is one of the best illustrations of faith I ever encountered.

He was saying in effect that he could not tell what the future was. Neither can we. It might be raining or sunny, it might be difficult or easy; it might be pleasant or unpleasant. No one, as the prayer has it, knows what a day may bring forth. That boy was saying that whatever happened, someone would provide him with "shelter from the stormy blast" and he would trust that and go on his way.

You are aware, I hope, that faith is not just a matter of religion but of life itself. Science lives by faith and so does politics. We do not know enough to put in your eye and we could not live twenty-four hours on the basis of our knowledge. We are always venturing out beyond the facts and daringly trusting our lives and fortunes to what we believe but cannot prove. The little boy had it right. Whatever happens, God will provide, and it is for us to do our duty and trust Him. That is one reason we call it the Christian "faith."

George Washington at the Constitutional Convention put this same idea in more classic English. We have forgotten, I fear, how desperate was the American situation when those fifty-five men gathered in Philadelphia in 1787. The Articles of Confederation had proved to be a weak reed with no central authority. Colonial jealousies appeared in the deliberations, and it looked as if the American experiment would end in failure. The delegates were not of one mind, and hovering over the whole meeting was the specter of public opinion and public reaction. In one of the difficult times when the Convention threatened to break up, the chairman, George Washington, spoke some great words to the delegates. He told them that it was probable that nothing they adopted would be approved and that perhaps another dreadful conflict was to be endured. But, he added, if to please the people they offered what they themselves disapproved, how could they afterward defend their work? Then he spoke these great words: "Let us raise a standard to which the wise and the honest may repair. The event is in the hand of God."

The Christian layman is a fellow who decides to act on the basis of the promises God has made us in Christ. Best of all, the more we experiment with them the surer we become of their truth and validity. Amen!

Format by Katharine Sitterly
Set in Linotype Electra
Composed and printed by York Composition Co., Inc.
Bound by The Haddon Craftsmen, Inc.
HARPER & ROW, PUBLISHERS, INCORPORATED